FUN

and

Verse

by

Robert Ford

PublishAmerica
Baltimore

First printing

PublishAmerica has allowed this work to remain exactly as the author intended, verbatim, without editorial input.

ISBN: 978-1-4489-8081-9
PUBLISHED BY PUBLISHAMERICA, LLLP
www.publishamerica.com
Baltimore

Printed in the United States of America

This is dedecated to my family and friends
for their love and support especially
Kathy, Kelly, Brian, Elaine Ford, Joan McGinley

A special thanks to Maria Zander for helping me
retype some of these poems.

Humor

AN IRISH POEM

I want to write a poem about the wearing of the green.
I know that I can do it because I have the Irish gene.
Maybe I should write something about the Emerald Isle.
Something that I know would make an Irish person smile.

I could go way out on a limb, maybe take a chance
and write about the guy they call "Lord of the Dance."
I know a lot about the Irish, to show you what I mean.
An anorexic Irish prostitute is known as Tramp O'Lean

Here's some more Irish history I feel I should report.
You can't get cash from a leprechaun, because they're always short
If some more knowledge about Irish history is what you're after
An Irishman is only happy when he's Dublin over with laughter

Irish I wouldn't have started this because it really isn't funny
When my mind gets into this mode, everything has to come out punny.
So instead of writing a lovely poem about the Irish folk,
This has turned into a disaster that is nothing but a joke

OFF TO SEE THE WIZARD

I am a lonely scarecrow in the middle of the field.
Wondering what this day is finally going to yield.
I'm here in the Land of Oz, a pole stuck up my behind.
Since I don't have a brain, I can't say that I mind.

I hear a girl with a dog, singing down the lane.
She's off to see the Wizard, maybe I can get a brain.
We continue down the road made of yellow stone,
Over on the side, there's a Tin Man all alone.

So we ask him what is wrong and he begins to start.
How happy he would be if he only had a heart.
"Why not come along with us and see the Wizard too,
Maybe if you're lucky he'll give a heart to you."

As we follow Dorothy and Toto her tiny dog.
We come across this Lion who seems to be agog.
We start walking toward him but as we were getting near.
He started crying and to shake from some inner fear.

"We're going to see the Wizard, why don't you come along,
Maybe he can give you courage and you can feel strong."
Happily we dance and sing down the road of yellow brick.
We didn't see the oil spill that made the road real slick.

That's when Dorothy's dog falls and Dorothy trips and flips,
The Lion then flies over her, and the Tin Man slips.
I've no brain so I don't stop and nearly break my neck.
We went off to see the Wizard but had a Toto wreck

MY DISASTER DATE

One day when I was way down yonder in New Orleans
I saw this pretty woman in some very sexy jeans.
As pretty as any calendar girl I have ever seen
She seems like she's a wild one, you know the kind I mean.

Her Retriever beside her, looks like she's full of puppy love.
but I couldn't help but notice that she wore a latex glove.
I felt it's now or never so I asked her for a date
We could be walking the dog together, wouldn't that be great!

As we walked I told her, I know everybody's somebody's fool
I asked, "Why the glove?" She said, "So I can pick up Bruno's stool"
"I'm sorry are you saying you pick up your doggie's poo?"
"Yes, and if your do not have a glove it gets stuck on you."

She said she has some in her purse because you never know,
when Bruno will get that sudden urge and he'll have to go.
He does the loco-motion and gives his bod the twist,
then he lifts his rear leg up and I get truly pissed.

My Venus in blue jeans tells me that her name is Sherry.
I tell her she's the kind of gal I think that I could marry.
She cried, "You talk too much, what is going through your head.
We just met an hour ago. Now you want to wed?"

I grab Bruno's leash from my new favorite lass,
he begins to gallop and drags me on my ass.
I hope he decides to stop, and I mean real soon,
cause if he doesn't I'll be showing people a blue moon

Hey, girl, I am sorry, I know breaking up is hard to do.
But after what just happened I need to get far away from you.
My butt cheeks are deep purple and I'm in so much pain
I need some drugs so I'll be able to walk like a man again

Though this poem makes this sound recent, it was several years back.
I hurt my rear end so badly, it still has a big crack
The moral of the story, don't pick up girls in the park my friend,
because if you do, I promise, you will regret it in the end.

THE GIFT

My kitty cat Samantha is knocking on my back door.
She brings something into the house and sets it on my floor.
What is this thing that the cat's brought into my little house,
is it just a raw hot dog or the body of a mouse?

I shoo the cat away with the end of a kitchen broom.
I hurry back to check what she brought into the room.
I wasn't quite sure what it was, I really must confess.
But I got a little worried when I saw a tiny dress.

Maybe it's a little doll that she found in the back yard,
since it's all chewed up identification's kind of hard.
If I go to pick it up with nothing on my hand,
and it turns out to be a mouse, I'm not sure where it'll land.

I get a plastic bag and pick it up like doggie poo,
and throw it in the garbage. There's nothing left to do.
The more I thought about it, the question that arose,
was why someone would dress up a mouse in little clothes.

As we sit here in the living room, I'm feeling like a louse.
Then the ghost of Walt Disney say's my cat's done in Minnie Mouse.
I'll have to watch Samantha now, 'cause she's kind of tricky.
I don't want to find out later on that she's done in Mickey

EARS TO YA

A friend of mine told me your ears and noses always grow.
As soon as she mentioned this, my heart was filled with woe.
I rushed off to the doctor to see if this was true.
I am filled with panic and am not sure what to do.

I told him some of the stories of when I was a kid.
He said they could not happen, I said, "Oh yes they did.
You see when I was in high school I was very small.
I remember being just over five-foot tall.

The other problem was, I never weighed a whole lot.
Maybe one hundred twenty pounds was the most I got.
My parents always warned me don't go out without a cap,
and try to get inside quickly if your ears begin to flap.

I told them I do not wear a hat, that would not be cool.
I looked them in the eye and said, "Do you think you raised a fool?"
It was in the Winter of '64 when the snow was two feet high,
when this young man named Robert Ford got his first taste of sky.

While shoveling snow hatless, a gust of wind took me off my feet.
It sent me into the air and I went flying hard across the street.
Ever since that happened it caused some irrational fears,
to this day I don't leave the house without something on my ears.

And then besides my ears, I have a nose that I despise.
It looks just like Pinocchio's after he told all his lies.
Not only is my nose long, it's also very wide.
When my kids were younger, they would use it as a slide.

Now that I have grown up and put on some extra weight,
the chances of me taking off are not quite as great.
If I'm not careful on a very windy day,
I can start to teeter and begin to sway.

The answer to your question sir, is a definite no.
Once you have grown up those parts no longer tend to grow.
There are some of you out there laughing without really knowing,
my ears are so aerodynamic they're registered with Boeing.

AT THE DENTIST

Sitting in the dentist chair, my mouth already filled with pain,
the dentist has the nerve to ask if I want some Novocain
I said, "Yes, please give me some, then give me a little more,
unless you want to see me running out the exit door."

I know that I need the drugs, when they do their dental thing,
with all the crowns I have in my mouth I should be a king.
Those dirty rotten scoundrels, all put in with my consent,
cost me so much money, I can't afford to pay my rent.

The only tooth in my mouth that has not been repaired,
is way the hell back in there, as if anybody cared.
I call this tooth "The lonely guy" since it's all by itself.
And when they finally take it out, I'll put it on a shelf

When I hear my tooth start singing "Why not take all of me,"
it tells me that I'm drugged up as much as I want to be.
It occurs to me the dosage might be a bit too strong,
when the stupid dentist gets up and starts to sing along.

The dentist starts to do a dance and move all around the floor.
I need to tightly shut my eyes I don't wanna see no more.
I can only wait for the dentist to resume his work.
So I lean back and patiently await to feel the jerk.

AT THE DENTIST PART 2

I went back to the dentist to get a root canal.
He said he wouldn't hurt me, he said I was his pal.
He filled me up with Novocain, the idiotic fool,
the only thing that I could do was just sit back and drool.

He said he had a theory he would like to try out on me.
He told his nurse to blindfold him so he could not see.
"I don't think it's possible for you to try and drill,
won't you please let me up, I think I am getting ill"

Lifting up on his blindfold, he said," I think I can."
I said, "But if you're wrong, I become a holey man."
Wide-eyed he said, "Sit back, relax, take a breath and chill,
I promise I won't do anything that's against your will."

"You're planning to drill my tooth while you are totally blind"
My mouth full of saliva, I splash, "Are you out of your mind?
What if you make a mistake and drill deep into my head?"
He starts laughing funny and says, "I guess that you'll be dead."

It's at this point I realize his mind has turned to Jell-O.
Wanna know how scared I was? My body turned bright yellow.
As my body starts to quiver and my knees get weak,
he is getting so excited he can hardly speak.

So I jump up and smack him squarely in the face,
as he goes stumbling backwards, out the door I race.
His partners should fire him, he really is a quack.
If they don't do something I don't think I'm coming back.

AT THE DENTIST PART 3

I'm developing a toothache that's tender to the touch.
I need to find a dentist soon because it hurts so much.
I can't go back to the old one knowing he's such a klutz.
I won't go to his partners, I've decided they're all nuts.

I'll call that 800 number and use whom they recommend,
maybe he'll be gentle, someone that I can call a friend.
I get a number for Georgia Peach, likely a girl from the south.
I wouldn't mind having some Southern Belle looking in my mouth.

So I wait in the office, till they guide me to the chair,
when I hear the dentist come in, all I can do is stare.
Looking at this Georgia Peach makes me feel I want to cry,
'cause this particular Georgia Peach turns out to be a guy.

He says, "I need you to open your mouth up real wide.
That way I can take a look at what's going on inside."
He leans over, my eyes tear up, as I smell his breath.
It reeks so bad I feel that I'm facing certain death.

"I need to get a x-ray 'cause two crowns have sprung a leak.
We'll probably have to put in a bridge, there beside your cheek."
"About how much will it cost?" What he says makes me quiver,
"Where are you putting up this bridge, the Mississippi River?

"There's not enough of either tooth to put on another crown.
I hate to say this Mr. Ford, both these teeth are going down."
As my eyes start to glaze over, much to my surprise,
I notice little dollar signs forming in his eyes.

"I'm putting wax inside your mouth so I can make some gold."
Laughing quite hysterically he says, "I mean make a mold."
"Please sit down before you leave and fill out an application.
Make sure you give us the proper insurance information."

I filled out all the forms, then the girl said something odd.
"When would you like to come back and schedule with our God."
To say this makes me nervous, I really can't deny,
but in fact I stain my pants as I turn and say good-bye.

AT THE DENTIST PART 4

Dr. Peach himself calls me up and wants me to come in.
The way his words are slurring it's sounds like he's full of gin.
He says, "I have to pull those teeth, they really have to go."
I said, "Why don't you tell me something I don't already know."

I walk into the office and they sit me in the chair.
Then they proceed to act as if I wasn't there.
The appointment was at ten o'clock, it's now ten thirty-five.
I ask the receptionist if Doctor Peach is still alive.

"He drank a lot of coffee but he needs another cup,
he has to drink a bunch of it if he wants to sober up."
I don't know if she noticed how the blood rushed from my face.
I know she didn't notice that my heart began to race.

I won't let him work on me drunk, that's where I draw the line.
Once he gets more java in him, he'll probably do just fine.
I hear someone fall in the back, again I stain my pants.
I'm getting my ass out of here, soon as I get the chance.

I quickly make a run for it, my head gets really knocked.
For how the hell was I to know the front door would be locked.
Doctor Peach and his nurses help me in the chair.
I slowly start to feel the raising of my hair.

Despite all my worries he is finished pretty quick,
then I hear him mutter, "I think I may be feeling sick."
He rushes to the bathroom where I hear him heave.
After a few moments I feel the need to leave.

I figure it's all over so I pay the doc his fee.
Then I hear him laughing, "Oops, there's been a mistake by me.
I just pulled the wrong teeth, what an error on my part!
It seems I have been looking at another person's chart.

Now that I have figured out that your name is not Bob Ridge,
I feel kind of funny 'cause you didn't need that bridge."
He has the nerve to look at me, as he fumbles with the graph.
Seeing this is all my fault, I'm only going to charge you half.

I'm gonna do another search and find a lady Doc,
someone who can do the job, and not put me deep in hock.
I guess it wouldn't hurt too much, if she were really hot,
but if I can't accomplish this, I think I'll just let them rot.

AT THE DENTIST PART 5

I look through the yellow pages for a dentist that's a girl.
I find Dr. Mary Yankum, I think I'll give her a whirl.
I make a late appointment and behold who could ask for more.
I spy this black haired beauty queen who dresses up like a whore.

As I look at this woman, I picture dentists past,
I'm thinking to myself, "Bob, you've found a home at last!"
The assistant at the front desk says the Doc's a fitness nut,
and I should be careful not to let her see my rounded gut.

So as a precaution I suck my tummy in real tight.
The only problem I have now is that I can't breathe right.
As she begins to lower the back of my chair down,
she says, "Looks like your old dentist was working on a crown.

So if it's okay with you, I'll just start from there."
My only thought right now is how to get some air.
"Looks like you spend a lot of time at the local deli,"
I start to laugh, and just like toast, up pops my big belly.

I ask her to administer a lot of Novocain,
She says that it's her theory if there's no pain, no gain.
"I am not asking you to give my teeth some exercise."
I feel that old look of fear is coming back into my eyes.

I feebly say to her, "Just give me some laughing gas."
"If you think that you'll get some here you can kiss my ass."
I feel like I'm floating somewhere on the fabled River Styx.
"Didn't anyone here tell you that I'm a dominatrix?"

This is not exactly what I want to hear,
pulling out her whip, she grins from ear to ear.
I ask the Lord, "Why, me?" and I begin to choke.
A voice from up above says, "Can't you take a joke?"

She says, "Mr. Ford it's becoming very clear,
that for some strange reason you want out of here."
"I do not want to be whipped or for that matter spanked,
I just want an oral surgeon to get these teeth all yanked."

AT THE DENTIST PART 6

I'm going to Doctor Phil D. Mouth, an oral surgeon pro.
I sit down, pointing at my teeth, saying these all have to go.
"Mr. Ford, I can't pull these teeth, it's against my dental code."
"You'd better start doing something Doc, I'm in a fighting mode."

"I can't pull out your teeth Bob, they are really not that bad."
Finding a dentist with scruples now, really makes me mad.
"All I want is some falsies that is all I'm urgin'"
"Does it look like I'm some silly plastic surgeon?"

"Can't you put in some new plates? That's what I really want to see."
"Sir, take a good look around, do you see any pottery?"
"Doc, all I'm looking for is a perfect set of false teeth."
"I can't pull the old teeth out and they won't fit underneath."

I pick up the little walking stick he had by the door.
I hit it up against his head and knocked him to the floor.
I didn't want to kill him but wanted him to feel my pain.
I guess deep inside I just wanted to raise a little cane.

The nurse goes out and calls the police, she really has some nerve.
They come and put handcuffs on me, something I do not deserve.
For the attack on Doctor Mouth, they were gonna cook my goose,
after I explained what happened, teary-eyed they turn me loose.

I walked up to this big boxer and gave him the high sign,
figuring when he hit my teeth, he'd knock out at least nine.
He came back and bit my ear saying, "You are going to die, son."
Wouldn't you know with my luck, I'd go and pick Mike Tyson.

I call him big sissy man, knowing his feelings would be hurt.
He rears back, hits me in the teeth, and I land up in the dirt.
I search my bleeding mouth, only to find I only lost one tooth.
When Dr. Mouth said they were in there good, he must have told the truth.

THE CLONE

I'm looking at this new machine where you can make a clone.
Maybe I can learn to use it so I won't be alone.
The more I think about it, this machine I am gonna steal
I need to know if this really works, is this thing for real?

I take and hide it in my den, and cover it with a sheet,
now I need to find the perfect mate to make my clone complete.
I see my pet Iguana, Margaret, step into the box,
the door closes tightly, then automatically it locks.

I try to open up the door by using a crowbar,
I work so hard I start to sweat but I don't get too far.
I try like heck to break the iron door apart,
my hand hits the button and makes the damn thing start.

The machine starts smoking, then bounces up and down,
the next thing I know is it's going round and round.
The thoughts running through my head are nothing but obscene,
could this journey Margaret's on, make her a human being.

I hear a voice coming from inside this big machine,
apparently somewhere inside was a human gene.
I wait outside the door as she undergoes the change.
I am wondering what she'll look like, this is very strange.

As I'm looking at the door, I think I see some motion.
There is the new Margaret, that's some kind of magic potion.
To those who don't like human cloning, I don't mean to perturb.
But there is only one word to describe it, that word is superb.

The woman standing there has a pretty body and great tail,
the scariest thing on her is each and every fingernail.
I don't know how good she will be when we go to bed,
but with that long tongue of her's, she's got to give great head.

Her arms and legs are kind of short but she's over 5 foot tall,
except for the light green tint to her skin, she's cute overall.
As for intelligence, I'm not looking for any wizard.
I don't really expect too much, she did come from a lizard.

THE CRUISE

I went on a Singles Cruise to find myself a mate,
if I don't get lucky it'll be one expensive date.
Looking for a pretty woman, I search up and down the deck.
I sit down to take a rest and feel soft lips upon my neck.

The girl that does all this kissing is a beautiful brunette.
She says her name is Nancy and she's not playing hard to get.
It's a walk to remember as we stroll hand in hand,
everything is going exactly as we had planned.

We dance, play games and do all that other fiddle-faddle,
and end up watching the chick flick "Sleepless in Seattle"
Nancy's so tan and beautiful, I ran up and kissed her,
I don't stay by the pool to long otherwise I blister.

We went to a costume party, since it was Halloween,
she went as a fairy princess, I went as a drag queen.
I hate to admit it but I have to confess,
I looked rather stunning in my red sequenced dress.

Feeling life is wonderful we go back to my room.
Little did we know about the impending doom.
All of a sudden we get knocked right out of the bed,
she lands smack on her fanny, while I land on my head.

We get dressed, run up on deck, to find we hit a rock,
now the boat is sinking, we are in a state of shock.
Look at the name of the boat, the owner doesn't have a clue
no one in their right mind would ever name a boat Titanic II.

A BAD DATE

As I turn on my computer, it tells me, 'You've got Mail'
When I see who it is from, it is opened without fail.
It's a tape from this sexy girl I know, and she's really getting down.
She wants to meet for some dirty dancing at a bar we have in town.

I put on a pair of real tight pants and a sexy shirt,
as we do our dirty dancing my body starts to hurt.
She sways her curvy body and says she's never been kissed.
We both know that that is a lie, but how could I resist.

These pants are tighter than I thought, I feel I might explode.
I should have known this outfit couldn't handle such a load.
All I know is, if there is any way I'm going to live,
with the way the pressure keeps building, something's got to give.

I don't know if I can stand the pain as I'm waiting to exhale.
I hope to keep my stomach in but I'm afraid to no avail.
I feel any moment there is going to be a blast.
I have got to do something, and I have got to do it fast.

All of a sudden, there are clothes flying everywhere.
I look at my friend and see my pants are in her hair.
There was too much pressure coming from my stomach heading south.
I have to say, I just gave my date, a good belt in the mouth.

LOST RELATIVES

I went over to Ireland to find my relatives,
they took one look at my red face and said to me, "What gives?"
I'm taken to a pub, where they buy me some ale.
I get so liquored up, that I land up in jail.

My long lost relatives bail me out, to them it's like a hobby.
I hate to say they're drunks, but they know the first name of their Bobby.
As we walk out of the jail, they hear my pockets jingle,
"It sounds like you have money, apparently you're single."

I go back into my room so I can again rinse off my face.
You see last night I came onto a girl who had a can of mace.
I told them I don't drink that much, last night was just a fluke
I normally do not drink so much that I have to puke.

If you want to be an Irishman, let us make this clear,
you have to start drinking and it must be more severe.
If I do that much drinking, I will become a bum,
then your new cousin will end up living in a slum.

I still want to be Irish but I can't drink that much.
So if I embarrass you, I'll leave but keep in touch.
Hugging all my new relatives, I'll leave them with a smile,
find a cab, hop on a plane and depart the Emerald Isle.

I'm sitting in my apartment back in the U.S.A.,
thinking of my new Irish friends, who live so far away.
I had to call them up to say I finally have atoned,
I put some pebbles in my drink so I can say I'm stoned.

THE GUITAR

I love to play on my guitar, morning,noon, and night.
I strum on it with my left hand, I never use my right.
I like all kinds of music, Classical, Jazz and Rock.
People love to hear me play up and down the block.

My fingers are quite nimble, you could say that they are quick,
I always use my fingers, very rarely use a pick.
I stand the guitar on end for show, then play on it with ease.
I'll even play your requested song, because I aim to please.

My favorites are Mathis tunes, they're filled with love and slow.
When I sing and play them, I often feel a certain glow.
But I'm not afraid to play some Bach or a Beatles tune.
Yes, I love to play on my guitar, morning, night and noon.

Sometimes I like to sing, as I play my favorite song,
inviting people with me to come and sing along.
I don't do it for the honor or even for the pay,
but the friendships that it helps build really makes my day.

I love to play on my guitar, noon, night and morning,
to my guitar-playing friends, I give you a warning.
You can either believe me or I think that I'm all wet,
but if you break a guitar string I don't want you to fret.

PARTY HARDY

I'm having a big clambake in the yard with all my friends,
and when Bobbo starts to party, the party never ends.
How am I able to party and rock around the clock?
This stone I found at San Quentin, it's called the jailhouse rock.

I love to dance to rock and roll and all that other stuff.
When it comes to booze and food I can never get enough.
As I sit in my chair drinking, I grin from ear to ear,
I feel quite affectionate from all the alcohol and beer.

I've been kissing all the women, they number in the dozens.
Since some of them are relatives, we now are kissing cousins.
I said I like to party all night but if the truth be told,
at the tender age of 62, I'm getting too damn old.

I've been drinking quite a bit, I'm really on a bender.
When I hear my girlfriend say to me, "Bob, please love me tender."
I said to her, "You bet I will" I thought I would surprise her.
For some reason, she lost the mood when I used tenderizer.

So if you see me dancing like Elvis and swiveling my hips,
don't be cruel and let nasty remarks slip from between your lips.
I have this real bad stomachache, I guess I have to pay my dues,
because of everything I drank tonight, I've got the G.I. Blues

THE DIET

I've gone on this fantastic new diet of bubble gum and beer,
how this diet actually works isn't really all that clear.
They say that you lose 20 lbs. in a little more than a week.
You're able to lose weight very fast if that is what you seek.

You think I'm farsighted and can't see the forest for the trees,
But the truth is I need to diet so I can see my knees.
You just chew wads of bubble gum instead of chewing food,
and blow lots of bubbles, even though that sounds kind of rude.

It's very important how you take your beer,
you just keep on drinking until your urine's clear.
This also makes you heave and be a little ill,
but since you can't keep food down, your calories are nil.

People who have done this are very big in the AA,
They note there may be a few setbacks but they will not say.
So if you are at a meeting and cannot tell who they are,
look for bubble gum on their face, it looks just like pink tar.

Their biggest problem is, since they can no longer drink the beer,
the fact they're going to regain the weight becomes very clear.
Maybe this diet is not going to be quite as great as I thought.
What am I going to do with the 20 cases of beer I just bought?

I guess I should also stop buying double bubble gum,
I'm not the brightest bulb in the box but I am not dumb.
I suppose I'll have to drink all that beer, go out on a bender.
By the time I finish, it won't matter if I'm fat or slender

KARAOKE NIGHT

Last night I went out drinking at the Old Showboat Saloon.
They had Karaoke there so I belted out a tune.
The people all are booing as I finish up my song,
if they think that would stop me they were absolutely wrong.

When I start singing Elvis songs, all of the people start to cry.
I feel there are many similarities between the "King" and I.
The woman in the front starts laughing as she wipes away her tears,
"The only thing you have in common is a big gut in later years."

I see a guy in a top hat come strutting through the front door,
his name is Simon Cowell and I've seen him somewhere before.
I think he is a talent scout who goes to karaoke bars,
to see if he can discover some bright future singing stars.

As I sing I start to dance like Travolta did in "Grease."
This talent scout yells out that he wants me right now to cease.
When I ask him what he thinks, he starts throwing crap up on the ceiling.
Luckily, he doesn't know how hard it is to hurt my feelings.

I thought he wanted me to stop, so he could say "a star is born."
As the crap falls on my head I'm starting to feel a bit forlorn.
The people grab my mike and throw me through the revolving door,
I don't think I'm ever going back to that place anymore.

AUTUMN

I want everyone to know that I have a good reason,
for not considering autumn as my favorite season.
It's not that I don't like the fall,
No, no, no that's not it at all.

That's when they start playing games in the NFL,
so when it comes to seasons I like it very well.
Many footballs flying everywhere,
with people out in the cool, crisp air.

"How can you not like autumn? Are you some kind of fool?"
The leaves start turning colors, kids go back to school.
When I was younger, my parents told me why each color glows.
Because God has the same magic brush he uses on rainbows.

The changing colors of the leaves always get me crying,
because it means those green leaves basically are dying.
So as they go from bright to brown,
those dying leaves fall to the ground.

When you look out the window, all your flowers and plants have died.
The beauty part is over now, and you want to stay inside.
But you go out, dig up the plants and stuff them in a bag.
With all the extra yard work you call Mom Nature an old hag.

With all the work, time for yourself is very hard to find,
you rush around like crazy, about to lose your mind.
It's when the leaves get so heavy that your lawnmower starts to bog,
You realize she's not a hag, but more like a female dog.

MY REVENGE

I'm sitting in the bathroom of this swank Mexican hotel,
and I do not mind telling you I really feel like hell.
I think I've lost my independency while sitting on the pot.
Because it looks like I am stuck here whether I like it or not.

I can't stop the fleeting movement coming from my rear end,
I should be leaving here soon to have dinner with my friend.
Every time I try to stand up, I have to sit right back down,
I'm starting to think I not going to make it into town.

The one thing I fear the most, is like most Fords, I'm filling up with gas.
I feel like 38-caliber bullets are shooting out my ass.
I can hear the water splashing in the toilet bowl,
hoping I don't break it has become my only goal.

I'm finally able to grab my phone and call the hotel staff.
I am hoping they can give me some help, but all they do is laugh.
The thing that bothers me the most is they do it with such zeal.
It's like they don't really give a shit exactly how I feel.

If this problem ever stops, you know "I will be back."
While I'm sitting on this john, I'm planning my attack.
I'll put a bunch of Ex-Lax in their drinks and also in their food,
then shut the water off to the hotel when they become unglued.

A few days have passed, my plan is in place,
you should see the look on each staffers' face.
I'm laughing now and my day is complete.
I've always believed that revenge is sweet.

A DAY IN THE SUN

It's the middle of the summer and the sun is very hot.
I forgot lotion on my belly, now it's a boiling pot.
I should never sunbathe because I know how it makes me feel.
I feel like a banana because I always start to peel.

Every time I go to the beach my body starts to burn,
I end up in the hospital, you think that I would learn.
I don't know why I go there, I hate the feel of gritty sand.
If I going to burn to death I'd rather do it on dry land.

I'd rather be at home, on the couch, watching a ball game,
then at some sandy beach with people sharing my last name.
To sing silly songs, around a fire, in the blazing heat,
to be quite honest with you, is not my idea of real neat.

My parents loved the sand and water, it's in my family tree.
In fact from what I understand that is how I came to be.
Yes, I was conceived in the sand, so it's not much of a reach.
The reason I'm so angry is that I'm a son of a beach.

AN EVENING WITH MOM

Sitting with my Mother in this old-time saloon,
it's got to be old-time, I see an old spittoon.
Drinking lots of Martinis we make ours both with gin.
As we continue drinking, it seems like we each grow a fin.

Although she has past her golden years many years ago,
when I go out drinking with my Mom we always feel a glow.
They painted the bar lavender on the walls and ceiling,
Whoever that idiot was could not have any feeling.

After she has had a few, Mom starts her barstool spinning.
When it comes to a contest of shame, I feel that I'm winning.
I hate to admit that I am also considered a Ford,
as she goes flying off the stool through some particleboard.

My mom is over eighty but they ask us to leave,
that's okay because these colors make me want to heave.
I go over and politely pick her body off the floor,
so once again my Mom and I go stumbling out the door.

My Mother starts to laugh, and she begins to fall,
she throws up everything she drank upon that awful wall.
From now on when she starts to drink I'm going to run for cover.
Even though she embarrasses me, I guess that I still love her.

Maybe if we walk down the street we can find my father.
He likes gin martinis too but I don't think we'll bother.
I'm getting kind of dizzy so I think I'll end this poem,
and try to sober up my Mom so I can get her home.

CALL ME MR. PRESIDENT

People say I'm crazy, a little nutty too.
I want to say, that absolutely is not true.
Just because my hair is gray and I dress a little weird,
I have not lost my sanity, if that is what you feared.

So my wife's name is Martha, this does not make me insane.
I call my wife Martha, because Martha is her name.
You say I may have lost my senses, fighting in the war.
I was fighting for my country, you hurt me to the core.

You say because I like to ride upon my white horse,
you're considering my mind may be a tad off course.
Whenever I call together my co-patriots and staff,
you people all look at each other and have a hearty laugh.

Go ahead and laugh, but you won't think it's so damn funny,
when you see my handsome face, stamped on some of your money.
Until you acknowledge who I am, you are tempting all the fates,
admit that I'm George Washington, President of the United States.

You're giving a jacket to me? Isn't that just great!
I'm sorry, what's that you said? You gave it to me straight?
You say you think I'm getting worse, as far as you can tell,
so you're going to make me go back into my padded cell.

BOWLED OVER

It was a hot, muggy, August day, with nothing much to do.
So some buddies and me decide to bowl a line or two.
We go to the alley, rent some shoes, and find a ball.
They put us next to some girls, we don't mind at all.

All the girls are very pretty and wearing these tiny shorts,
you can imagine the smiles between me and my cohorts.
I hadn't been bowling for number of years,
but I figured I'd improve after a few beers.

Since we all are staggering, the girls challenge us to a game.
We accept the challenge, the liquor makes us a touch insane.
The bet is 160 a game or 40 bucks a line,
we all look at each other and slur, "That'll do just fine."

As the match begins, the girls buy us all a drink.
I feel that's quite sporting of them, don't you think?
After a few beers and two pitchers of tonic and gin,
the boys are bowling terrific, looks like a certain win.

As we finish the 5th frame we are sixty pins ahead.
I feel like the rest of the guys, that these girls are dead.
Going into the beer frame, we can hardly see the pins,
all the guys are complaining how this bowling alley spins.

There is only one frame left and we are almost tied,
with all that we've been drinking I think our brains are fried.
Brian, our best bowler, is pretty drunk I'd say,
he keeps trying to bowl but he's four lanes away.

After all the pins are added we lose by a mere ten.
We turn over the money and I realize again,
it isn't the bowling that puts me in such a funk,
it's whenever I go bowling I get stinking drunk.

MONEY CAN'T BUY HAPPINESS

If I could change one thing by turning back the hands of time,
How would I express it, using just my words and rhyme.
I thought a lot about it and I cannot tell a lie,
I wish I knew back then, there's nothing money cannot buy.

Money can't buy happiness, which is what all the people say.
But I was never happy when there were bills I couldn't pay.
Were you real happy when the spousal fights sometimes got a little rough?
Were you fighting because you had too much money or didn't have enough?

Money can't buy love. Well, you might find this kind of funny,
how different people act, when they find out you have money.
They will be so nice to you and put up with all your shit.
They're hoping if they do, that you might give them some of it.

Money can't buy friendship. Here is where that theory falls,
Go and win the lottery, friends will come out of the walls.
The one thing money cannot buy, most certainly is health,
I would say you have far less stress, when you are blessed with wealth.

Some will say I'm cynical and must have a sorry life.
One thing I know for sure is, money means a lot less strife.
Look at the beauty in life, or a belief in God might cure your ills.
My friends, I believe in God and beauty, but they just don't pay the bills.

MY BOSS

I've decided I'm going to quit after 13 years of work.
No longer do I want to work for a boss who's a total jerk.
To cut myself off from this place I am making an incision.
I don't want anything to make me go back on my decision.

My boss is going to be surprised is all that I can say,
When he gets the two weeks' notice I'm handing in today.
I know he's going to ask me why I want to leave this job,
I'll tell him to his face I'm tired of working for a slob.

He fell downstairs, hurt his knee, now he wants someone to blame.
He yells at me, "You're not out to hurt, you are out to maim."
He really is so stupid I mean a real putz,
Trying to blame someone else when he is just a klutz.

To tell you the honest truth he's really nothing but a fool,
The only way to describe him is a synonym for mule.
The way he handles money is nothing but a crime,
He goes out and spends it all and I don't get a dime.

He doesn't compensate me what I think I deserve,
This idiot boss of mine has quite a bit of nerve.
Somebody should teach him the full sanctity of truth,
And the language that he uses almost is uncouth.

Maybe I should be more grateful, 'cause deep down he's a nice guy.'
I suppose I'll give him another chance, just don't ask me why.
There is one little tiny thing that still makes me quite annoyed.
I realize slugging down a drink, that I am self-employed.

MY LOTTERY TICKET

It is raining here in Illinois, isn't that just ducky,
I'm sitting here in my little truck, wishing I were lucky.
I ask Lady Luck to watch over me, I'm hoping that she will,
'cause the Wisconsin Lottery is worth 250 mil.

The front of my truck is shaking, I may have a flat.
I have got to stop my truck, right where it is at.
When I got outside the truck, I knew my brain was fried.
I thought how lucky I am, it's flat on just one side.

So I get my jack out and fix it, in the pouring rain.
The hail pounding on my head, is driving me insane.
As I get back into my truck, I'm soaking wet,
I'm thinking all the while, how lucky can I get.

The time is passing quickly, it's starting to get late.
The place where I buy the tickets, closes right at eight.
I'll need to speed the truck up, so I can get there when I planned.
I didn't know about a monsoon season in Chicagoland.

While I'm driving up here, I need to go by the zoo,
To see if the animals are walking two-by-two.
If I notice that they are, this truck I am going to park,
I want to be there with them when they go into the ark.

I don't know what I did wrong, there must be some mistake,
'cause the road I'm driving on, has turned into a lake.
As I look out of my truck, on this rainy day,
I see all my hopes and dreams, slowly wash away.

I pull into the parking lot, they're about to close the door.
I yelled at them, "Don't close it yet maybe you can take one more."
Running on wet pavement, I slipped and fell on my fat ass,
And as my feet go flying up, they break the front door glass.

They went and called the cops on me and best that I can tell,
I'll be spending most of the night in a tiny jail cell.
I didn't get my Lotto ticket, but I'll probably get a fine,
And with the way my luck is running I'll probably do some time.

It is raining here in Wisconsin, isn't that just ducky.
I'm sitting in this little cell, wishing I were lucky.
It is apparent Lady Luck does not seem to care,
Whether or not, I become, a multi-millionaire.

THE ACCIDENT

I'm driving in my sports car stepping on the gas,
flying by at eighty, I spot this lovely lass.
Looking at this pretty woman, I begin to pant.
I really want to stop but find out that I can't.

My car starts to skid like the street is filled with grease.
Looking down I realize that my brakes won't release.
Now this car is moving around like a spinning top,
God only knows where this damn car is going to stop.

As I spin, my arms and legs are flying all about.
If it weren't for my seat belt, I'd be flying out.
Now because of all the movement, I make matters a lot worse,
I grab the gearshift by accident and throw it in reverse.

Suddenly the brakes let go and tires start to squeal.
You have no idea of the panic that I feel.
Oh great, now the gas pedal's stuck, that's just what I need.
The car starts going backwards at a high rate of speed.

When I was in the navy, a rocking boat would make me sick,
I get that same feeling as I run into that pretty chick.
When the car finally hits her, she doesn't fly too far.
Luckily I run over her with only half my car.

The car makes an abrupt stop as it runs into a house.
I don't think I have to tell you, I'm feeling like a louse.
As they put me into the ambulance I just start to doze,
because of all the medication, my eyes begin to close.

I wake up in my room with a sprained wrist and broken leg.
I decide to ask the girl out, I may have to beg.
Searching the whole hospital I eventually find her room.
I bring her a dozen roses and a bottle of perfume.

"You are such a beauty, can I ask you out for a date,
or can you give me a reason why I should have to wait?"
Lying in her body cast with her mouth tightly wired shut,
she gives me the finger and mumbles, "You, sir, can kiss my butt."

THE CABBIE

I'm walking down the street one day when it begins to rain,
it's coming down in pellets and I start to feel pain.
When these ice pellets hit me I can feel a little jab,
I think something is trying to tell me I should hail a cab.

The cabbie that pulls to the curb is really quite obtuse,
he won't open up the door even though all hails broke loose.
"Hey there, taxi driver, open up the freaking door,
these pellets are coming down even harder than before."

I see a touch of evil come into his beady eyes,
and he flips me the middle finger much to my surprise.
The welts forming on my body are giving me much pain,
I'm thinking to myself I stopped a cabbie who's insane.

I feel that my anger has finally begun to show,
as I pick up the bus stop sign and break his rear window.
The cabbie starts to panic as I express just how I feel,
saying, "I'm going to kill that crazy man behind the wheel."

Before I'm able to do this I'm tackled from behind,
I believe this guy is going to try and change my mind.
A second man jumps on me as the cabbie speeds away,
the 3rd man who arrives asks if he can help me out today.

As I finally start to calm down I answer, "Yes, you can.
I'm late for an appointment but I've come up with a plan.
I don't want to have to flag down another crazy cab,
So maybe you could drive me to my alcohol rehab."

The only memento I have is the cabbie's license plate,
maybe I'll be able to run him down, wouldn't that be great!
As I'm sitting here a lovely thought comes rushing to my head,
"Forget the stupid rehab, take me to a nice bar instead."

THE CONTEST

I have a good friend named Ursala, who is a little dumb.
She's 51 years old and obsessed with beans and bubble gum.
She read about a contest, who could blow the biggest bubble,
"I've blown a bubble two feet wide, but that I'll need to double."

She said she'd dedicate the contest to her boyfriend Dan,
but that she would keep the Grand Prize, a brand new Chevy Van.
I'm afraid she will eat some beans before she goes on stage,
if she does I hope she douses them with a bunch of sage.

I feel her sense of humor is a little bit shy of strange,
that may be over doing it but I think I'm in the range.
She took a wad of bubble gum and spread it over her ass,
then started heavy farting and made a bubble with the gas.

As the contest begins, in her mouth, go forty sticks of gum,
in fact the final five sticks, have to be pushed in with her thumb.
She says, "I'll start chewing so I can blow big ones for my beau."
I said, "Big ones from your mouth or ass is all I want to know."

You probably shouldn't have eaten those 4 big cans of beans.
It might make you quite gassy and we all know what that means.
She starts to blow a bubble and it grows to eight feet wide.
When the wind starts blowing harder, she teeters side to side.

Another gust of wind comes and she goes flying in the air,
the bubble comes out of her mouth and gets tangled in her hair.
Then the worst thing happens, she begins to fart,
left and right, up and down, she begins to dart.

She kept going upward and started heading West,
she became a legend about this I don't jest.
We know that she is living and we know she is not dead,
she's our local UFO, Ursala Floating Overhead.

THE DREAM

I need to speak to the sandman about some reoccurring dreams,
I wanted to see if this nightmare is as crazy as it seems.
I am dressed in a sailor suit that makes me look quite silly,
the color of it's orange and purple and it's kind of frilly.

I'm sitting on a small boat rocking up and down,
if it ever stops I'm heading straight into town.
So I head into this seaport looking for a drink.
As I'm walking down the street this suit starts turning pink.

Turning into a speakeasy the doorman stops me cold,
"May I ask you where you're going? If I may be so bold."
"I'm going to get drunk on a bottle of your best gin,"
"That's going to be hard 'cause I'm not gonna let you in.

You're not coming in here till you've undergone a change,
It looks like you might have lice and possibly the mange.
You need to go, take a bath and get a change of clothes,
the smell that you are giving off irritates my nose."

These comments hurt my feelings even though they are true,
I'm hoping that this pink suit turns a more manly blue.
This is what I'm dreaming when I suddenly wake up.
I go and make some coffee and pour myself a cup.

I prefer to think that my mind if fairly sane,
and that there is nothing wrong with my current brain.
But I still can't figure out why I have this silly dream,
if I don't find out pretty soon, I think I'm going to scream.

The psychiatrist I went to says my mind is still okay,
just because you dream in pretty colors doesn't mean you're gay.
When I see the sandman I am going to throw a fit,
it probably won't bother him, he's got a lot of grit.

ANOTHER BAD DREAM

I had the strangest dream last night, it was really weird.
I'm living in Hawaii and have somehow grown a beard.
That's not so bad but in this dream I'm getting on a boat,
when I am in the real world I won't get on a float.

So I'm sailing on this schooner somewhere out near Maui.
The mast swings around, hits my head, giving me an owwie.
The injury, said all the crew, was looking pretty grave.
They all had their doubts my life they would be able to save.

While lying on the deck I spot a female kangaroo,
she is sporting a Mohawk and a sinking boat tattoo.
She says that she is royalty, in fact, she is a queen.
But she's the most outrageous kangaroo I've ever seen.

The next thing I know we're below deck and sitting on a couch.
She reeks to high heaven, because she has onions in her pouch.
"Queenie" puts a balloon on her butt and fills it up with gas.
I'm praying very hard that gas is all that she will pass.

She has on a petticoat searching the fridge I see
I said, "Help yourself to some cheese. I have lots of Brie."
A cow with pants comes in and asks if he can have a bite.
Seeing a cow and Roo in clothes means something is not right.

Suddenly I awake to the church bells ringing in the tower.
As I look at my watch, I've been asleep for about an hour.
I look back to figure out what this dream could mean.
It was downright gross and bordered on the obscene.

A kangaroo has lots of hops and cow is walking meat.
To figure out the rest is going to be quite a feat.
Petticoats and jeans could be wash and wear
that would explain to those two things but what about the hair?

As I go into this bar the bartender has a Mohawk on his skull.
He also has a tattoo of a ship but you only see the hull.
Suddenly everything to me has become undeniably clear.
I order two burgers with cheese and onions and wash them down with
beer.

ENCHANTED ISLE

I was sitting back this evening when a big smile came on my face.
My mind has taken me on a flight to a most romantic place.
I am on an island with the bluest waters I have ever seen,
and along with the pure white sand beaches I am feeling quite serene.

I'm sitting comfortably in this wonderful beach chair,
suddenly I get approached by a woman with long hair.
She's in a skimpy bikini so I know just what this means.
She, of course, has to be considered the woman of my dreams

She says her name is Ariel, but I'll get nothing from this sexy chick.
Because somehow my demented mind has put me in a Walt Disney
flick.
I go ahead and ask her if we're on some Enchanted Isle.
The only thing that she can do is crack a little smile.

"You're telling me I'm in a place where the creatures sing and dance.
If they expect me to join in, tell them they don't stand a chance."
The animals want a musical, based on the "Terminator."
She says the star is going to be, Arnie the Alligator.

I can hear the gentle thumping of beaver and otter tails,
meanwhile all the little fishes are practicing their scales.
The ducks are holding their heads high, so they're all quacking up.
A mother dog is tap dancing there, with her little pup.

By now I'm laughing so hard I think I may have a heart attack.
But I just have to hear the 'gator say the phrase "I will be back."
I begin to feel myself being rudely shaken,
if it doesn't stop real soon surely I'll awaken.

If this happens to wake me up I don't know what I'll do,
Maybe I can make it back before "Terminator 2."
Even if I don't return, one day I had a smile on my face.
All because my demented mind took me to a most romantic place.

THE FIGHTER

They call me "Bob the killer" and I fear no mortal man,
I'm known as a great street fighter, I do the best I can.
My hands are fast as Jackie Chan's, my feet are just like Bruce Lee.
When you put these two things together no one's as good as me.

There is a guy named Romeo who has an evil eye,
I don't want to sound like a hard ass but Romeo must die.
He says he's going to get me and put me in my grave.
'Cause I'm the only one who can put an end to his crime wave.

People can start to order their flowers from their local florists.
He's running up against someone who is meaner then Chuck Norris.
He tries to run me over in the middle of rush hour,
I jump and kick his windshield in, I give him a glass shower.

I have been known to kill a man with just a single blow,
Either coming from my rock hard head or my steel-like toe.
Even though my hair is gray I can still do fancy flips,
And my enemy's survival is at my fingertips.

Romeo gets an iron monkey and throws it at my head,
I'm starting to get the feeling that he wishes I were dead.
It bounces off my head and puts a hole into the wall,
I just stop and stare at him like it doesn't hurt at all.

We're in mortal combat now and he is in a lot of pane,
'Cause I threw him out the window, not to kill him, just to maim.
I've been in so many battles that I've gotten my share of nicks.
I love to fight karate style, it's the way I get my kicks.

THE NEWSMAN

Hi, I'm Bob, the anchorman, for the local evening news,
because I am so good at it they let me pick and choose.
They send me all the events that happened in the day,
I then look them over and decide what I should say.

Like the story of the pastor who serves breakfast every week,
I try to get a hold of him for the answers that I seek.
He gives me an answer but I think it's a lot of bull,
he says all he's really doing is keeping the faith full.

Next, along came Polly Ester who was looking for a hit man,
she put an ad in the paper but let me tell you what she ran.
She needed someone to get right up next to her and smack her,
because what she put in the ad was "Polly wants a whacker."

Then there's something about Mary, a prostitute in town,
who is telling a sad story about what's got her down.
You see, she's into bondage, so here is the new flash,
she says she's really mad 'cause she's always strapped for cash.

Sitting in my duplex apartment, looking at each new brief,
I realize is that this job is bringing me, nothing less than grief.
I need a bigger market or I will never see Bob Ford,
written on an Emmy or any other kind of award.

TOO HOT

It was steaming hot out and the air was just so damn dry,
there wasn't enough moisture to allow someone to cry.
It felt like you were walking in the desert heat.
If you went without shoes you'd likely burn your feet.

If you went without a hat, chances are, you'd burn your head.
If you went without water, you would probably wind up dead.
I'm telling you, it was such a weird sensation,
as you watched the birds walk to their destination.

It seemed to have the same horrible effect on cats,
they were lying down, right next to some dirty rats.
I have a dog, do you wanna know what happened to her?
She was out for just ten minutes and burned off all her fur.

It was hotter here than if you were sitting down in Hades,
You need to find a SPF somewhere up in the eighties.
I felt so sorry for my fair skinned sister,
one step outside and she began to blister.

If you bought an ice cream cone, whether you liked it or not,
It melted before you took 3 steps, it really was that hot.
You couldn't even cool off by jumping into the pool,
the water there was bubbling, you'd have to be a fool.

Even earthworms when they came up from the dirt
browned up like a steak, you know that had to hurt.
The people began to pray, "Lord, save us from this hell."
Whether he as listening, I really could not tell.

It really got me mad and I let out a mighty roar,
"Father, we need rain right now!" and then it began to pour.
My neighbors all fell to their knees and shouted out, "My Lord."
"You're making a big mistake, I'm not Him, my name's Bob Ford."

THE COWBOY GIVEAWAY

I saw this Cowboy giveaway and thought I'd buy a chance,
because if I'm the winner I'll spend two weeks at a ranch.
All I have to do is scratch this silver stuff off the card.
Hey, it says I am a winner! That wasn't very hard.

I know nothing about ranching, but the owners seem real nice.
I'm hoping that they will be helpful, and give me some wise advice.
I put on a pair of jeans, a shirt and brand new Stetson hat,
I look just like the great John Wayne except that I am so fat.

These people must be crazy, they want me to milk a cow.
I try hard to explain to them that I do not know how.
Grabbing this thing with both my hands, they tell me to go faster.
I tell them if I do that, it could be utter disaster.

They place me on this big steed, he promptly bucks me to the ground.
The owners run up yelling, "Would you please stop horsing around."
They ask me to gather up some eggs and you can plainly see,
I spilled the whole basket in my lap, I guess the yolks on me.

Asking me to rope a steer, I catch two and bring them in.
Considering how well I did I cannot help but grin.
I see the order for their slaughter written on the butcher's sheet.
I couldn't help but tell them "I knew you two were going to meet."

There was a goat swinging a golf club, he was filled with glee.
I asked the rancher what it was, he told me, a goat tee.
He sent me out to corral some sheep, the next thing that I knew,
I yell with an Italian accent, "I'm gonna catch a ewe."

The rancher's wife comes running in, "There's a stage among the herds"
I yell, "Damn, that always happens when I make a play on words."
They tell me they want me to go right upstairs and start to pack,
saying that they'll refund my money, but they never want me back.

RUSH IN LOVE

Rowing down the Mystic River in my little old canoe.
I'm feeling kind of lonely and wondering what I should do.
So I bring the boat back to the dock and put it in my car.
It's not in real solid but I don't have to go too far.

So I'm sitting at my computer desk laying out some plans,
knowing for certain I have to take things into my own hands.
(For those of you with dirty minds, I'm going to pause a sec.)
That thought crossed my mind too, but let's try to keep it in check.

I see this Russian lady named Olga on the internet.
She's just what I am looking for so I won't play hard to get.
I am not looking for love actually, I just want a perfect date.
If something more would become of this, she could turn out to be my
mate

The only thing about her is, her English isn't great.
That can be quite hairy sometimes when you communicate.
This can be a big problem, this lack of communication.
There are lots of words misunderstood or lost in translation.

She said she is with the KGB, now I'm thinking spy,
I found out it's a class that teaches English at the "Y."
We moved in together, I asked her to clean the windowsill.
She looked at me in horror, "Why do you want I should kill Bill?"

Now I have to explain I meant to wipe down the windowsill,
and there's no godly reason for her to kill our neighbor Bill.
A few months later I realized she was picked for me by fate,
The only thing left for me to do is propose and pick a date.

I give her the ring saying "I don't want to rush ya honey."
I start to laugh at this great pun because I think it's funny.
She starts yelling at me, "You monster, now you have gone to far.
I told you I'm never going back to the U.S.S.R.

She gets up, packs her two bags, and goes slamming out the front door.
"You want to send me back to Russia, I don't want you no more!"
Rowing down the Mystic River in my little old canoe.
Feeling I'm better off alone, then to try to start anew.

I LOVE CHEESE

There is absolutely nothing I love more than cheese,
just a little smell of it brings me to my knees.
I don't care if it be American or Swiss,
when it comes to eating cheese, you just cannot miss.

I put it on a sandwich or in a bowl of soup,
where it slowly melts and turns into delicious goop.
I love it when you stir it in some macaroni,
or take a piece of Brick cheese and put it on baloney.

I tremble when I put some cream cheese on a Ritz,
if I add peanut butter, I go into fits.
I can't think of a thing I like any better,
except for the taste of piece of good mild Cheddar.

I also like my Gouda and the creamy taste of Brie,
Limburger is the only cheese that does not appeal to me.
I'm not hard to get along with, I'm so easy to please.
Whenever you come to see me, just bring along some cheese.

A DAY AT THE BEACH

It's a summer of love so I took my girl to the beach.
Her name is Georgia Brown and she's as sweet as any peach.
Wearing her bikini she is as sexy as can be,
I'm going to describe her and I think that you'll agree.

Her bronze legs are outstanding, they are shapely and they're long.
Her well rounded bottom can really fill out any thong.
She has a loving face that always wears a winning smile.
This girl has plenty of class and she carries it with style.

Guys always check her over from the bottom to the top.
I know that this happens when I see all of their jaws drop.
We are quite the happy couple as we walk hand-in-hand.
Watching all of the people as they frolic in the sand.

There are people right in front of us, now I am not a prude,
but they are going at it to the point of being lewd.
Not to be obscene I'll use a different kind of lingo,
what they are doing now could be called beach blanket bingo.

There is a sign stuck in the sand and this is what it said,
"The Psycho Beach Party" is just a hundred feet ahead.
A surfer carrying his board seems like a real flake,
everybody knows they have no surf on this tiny lake.

The tattoo he has on his back, as far as I can tell,
seems to be a picture of the infamous Bates Motel.
This party is filled with wackos, even the surfer's wife,
I check them all out carefully to see if there's a knife.

There's a bunch of girls in bikinis showing off their skins,
giving lip locks to each other they must be kissing kins.
This is a bikini summer which makes me very glad,
It's called bikini summer 'cause some are good and some are bad.

THE DRIVING SCHOOL

Easy Method Driving School is where I can learn to drive.
I just want to go from here to there and make it back alive.
I look up in the phone book and find out their address.
How good they are at teaching is anybody's guess.

A friend of mine drives me there, so I can relax,
filling out the forms I just write down all the facts.
As my instructor sits me behind the wheel,
I just can't believe how wonderful I feel.

Looking to my right the instructor is in prayer,
when he looks back at me, he sees my nostrils flare.
As we are turning the corner, I see a big tow truck,
about to pick up a car that obviously was stuck.

Seeing an older woman crying in the driver's seat,
I notice it is a car from the Easy Driving's fleet.
Turning to the instructor I ask who the woman is.
He quickly snaps back at me, "That's none of your damn biz!"

As I start to strangle him, he yells out, it's my boss,
that's her fifth accident." He senses that I am cross.
I quickly jump out of the car and I start to cuss,
I really don't need a license, I'll just take the bus.

A NIGHT AT THE MOVIES

I go to the cinema to watch the picture show,
and sit behind some loud mouth, little did I know.
At first, I am nice and ask him please to shoosh.
He turns around and gives me a little push.

I ask him nicely to be quiet, I'm that kind of guy,
taking his middle finger he pokes me right in the eye.
It gets me a little madder, but I still try to be nice.
It seems the boob in front of me is not taking my advice.

The subtle hints I give him he would just ignore,
I hate to admit it but I am getting sore.
This gets me madder but my control prevailed,
if it hadn't, on his head I would have wailed.

He turns to his buddy and they start talking real loud,
disturbing not only me but everyone in the crowd.
I am getting tired of hearing his booming voice.
This leads me to believe I have got to make a choice.

One is just to sit here and try not to get mad,
the other is to hurt him, hurt him really bad.
So like the little M&M, I kick him in the head.
The way he goes flying forward I think that he is dead.

I find out he is not, of course, that is a big relief.
The only thing that happened is he lost most of his teeth.
People jump up to admire my feat, please excuse the pun.
They offer to pay for my seat, as thanks for what I have done.

His mouth looks like it could be sore for about a week.
If he is really smart, he should not try to speak.
Then I take off my boot and hit him you know where.
He screams like a banshee but I don't really care.

Not taking him to the hospital, suggests I have no heart.
But what am I to do, the second show is going to start.
We're very happy and feeling kind of groovy.
we can all lean back and just enjoy the movie.

After watching the movie, some stitches he might be needing,
I put my t-shirt in his mouth to help him stop the bleeding.
I walk him to his car, and say, "Sorry I had to put you through it."
Next time someone asks him to shut up my guess is that he'll do it.

A BAD TRADE

I went to e Bay looking to find a deal,
something very special, I'm looking for a steal.
It can be international or from around the block,
if the price is good enough I don't care if it's in stock.

Wait, a fantastic deal has just popped up on the computer screen,
there's a 50,000 dollar necklace for not a lot of green.
So I put up a bid to see if it would be topped,
The price starts going higher it just could not be stopped.

The way this price keeps changing is really quite obscene,
it's bouncing around so fast I need some Dramamine.
For this magnificent necklace I will not be outbid,
I need to go higher so that's exactly what I did.

They say I made the final bid, the necklace now is mine,
a diamond necklace for half the price makes me feel fine.
This gentleman said he will send the prize right to my front door,
using a special messenger and it won't cost anymore.

A few days later, there he was, package in his hand.
This is working out even better than I planned.
I feel that I should compensate him with a generous tip.
'cause if I don't, I feel that I could end up with a fat lip.

I put the necklace in my pocket, to give to my girl at lunch.
As soon as I sit upon it, the whole restaurant heard the crunch.
That polecat on e Bay sold a necklace made of pure glass,
I now have thousands of pieces of it riddling my ass.

I tell the paramedics what happened and how much I spent,
they started laughing so hard we almost had an accident.
The people in the E.R. acted exactly the same way,
I swear, never again, to do any business on e Bay.

I SPY

They call me Bobbo Ford, secret agent extraordinaire,
with the body of Adonis and a great head of hair.
You wouldn't know it to look at me, but I'm the kind of guy,
people who are in the know will tell you that I'm a famous spy.

There was a cryptogram about my foe, the evil Doctor No Good.
Using my quick eyes and mind I decipher he's somewhere in the hood.
I think he's the meanest man in the world, let me tell you why.
He steals candy from kids and babies, just to make them cry.

Yes, Doctor No Good is going to rue this day,
someone who is this rotten I must put away.
Misleading everyone I pretend I'm overweight and gray,
I do not like to do it but it's a game I have to play.

Dr. No Good takes a cone from a kid, then steals a lollipop.
He is kind of far way from me but I yell at him to stop.
Running fast I tackle him and on his face he wears a frown,
'cause as soon as he sees me I inform him he's going down.

No longer will he be able to premeditate a theft,
'cause when I get through with him I'll make sure he has nothing left.
I let him know that he is now a prisoner of this fine state,
he tells me he knew I was good, but he didn't know how great.

Now that he is locked up, on my tuba I'll play a song,
the little kids and babies will be free to sing along.
Adults the world over are grinning from ear to ear,
'cause I caught Dr. No Good they no longer have to fear.

I'm lying on the couch, beautiful women at my side.
and their undying love for me is difficult to hide.
Each girl in a bikini, gives me kisses and tender hugs.
Wait, they all are leaving, Doc must be taking me off the drugs.

THE PSYCHIC

I went to see this mind reader who was a psychic too,
I put my hand into her's and asked her to give her view.
She went into a hypnotic state and then began to stare,
put both her hands on her head and started pulling out her hair.

I asked her what my future would be, I was filled with fear.
She said that she saw something but it wasn't very clear.
I didn't want to tell her this place was a clip joint,
I told her to try harder and get more to the point.

She said she saw a Ford and it looked kind of tired.
She started doing the job for which she was hired.
She saw me sitting in what looked like a wheel chair,
that was just something else she felt that she could share.

I said my name is Bob Ford and I was feeling quite run down,
the thought of being in a wheel chair really makes me frown.
The vision she sees has something to do with a bad break,
that's when I start thinking this chick is nothing but a fake.

"You're a mind reader, tell me what I'm thinking, if you dare."
She said, "I'd be more than glad to, except there's nothing there."
I got up to leave and yelled at her, "Now you have gone to far!"
I opened the door to leave and was promptly hit by a car.

The brakes had failed on a new yellow Mustang Convert,
as I went flying to the street, I really got hurt.
As I sit in my wheel chair, the psychic seems aloof.
It goes to show how right she was and I am living proof.

THE RAFTING TRIP

I'm heading to Colorado with my son-in-law and son.
All of us guys getting together, out for some manly fun.
We're going white water rafting for the ultimate thrill,
and I must confess I'm starting to feel a little ill.

Our guide introduces us to two more couples in our group.
Then he explains how to raft, filling us in on all the poop.
All of these four people are looking very fit and trim.
I'm sure they're all thinking, "Would you take a look at him!"

The guide then takes us down to see our rubber river craft,
we kind of look at each other and ask him if he's daft.
"You're telling us you're going to put 8 people in this boat,
then add on some camping gear and this thing is going to float?"

He quickly reassures us so we hop into the raft,
I sat down facing the wrong way and everybody laughed.
As I turn around, my face is as red as a beet.
The guide pushes us from the shore using both his feet.

As we start going down the river, I feel a little rise,
then we have a little dip, which should really be no surprise.
I notice that the weather is starting to get bad,
I hope it doesn't ruin our day, that would make me mad.

First it just starts to drizzle, then becomes a downpour rain,
I suggest we go to shore, the guide laughs like he's insane.
We are now on a raging river bouncing up and down,
the way the raft is tossing I feel we're all gonna drown.

Flying from my seat, I land on the lady in the front,
she asks that I get off her lap, she's being pretty blunt.
I apologize profusely and jump right off of her,
promising if I have my way that never will recur.

We're rowing and we're steering, dodging every new boulder,
I'm not sure of any of us growing any older.
Brian and Rob look like they enjoy temping fate.
Me, I'm just praying that I don't become fish bait.

The rain has stopped and we come to a spot where the waters ease,
I turn and start yelling at the guide, "Let me out of this boat please."
The next set of rapids everyone is ready to attack,
I sit down and have a smoke saying, "I'll wait 'til you get back."

BAD VACATION

I had a month's vacation so I got into my car,
didn't know if I'd travel near, or if I'd travel far.
Maybe I'd go to the north country, maybe head out west.
I thought I'd just start driving, then decide what I liked best.

Flying down the highway at seventy miles per hour,
I start laughing hysterically, feeling drunk with power.
Looking into the rearview mirror, I saw an angry cop.
He had his siren blaring and was telling me to stop.

Suddenly my car starts to swerve, is this how my life ends?
I'm telling you, I was so scared, I wished I wore Depends.
My little car smashed hard into, a massive mountain of stone.
The impact sent funny vibrations through each and every bone.

A Wyoming cop yelled at me, "Have you been drinking too much wine?
Get your ass outta' that car, I'm going to make you walk the line."
I don't think I can do it, after being in that crash,
'cause blood had flowed into my eyes from where I hit the dash.

The next thing I remembered, I'm in a hospital bed,
with yards of white gauze tightly wrapped around my throbbing head.
I thought I should have gone to Munich, maybe, Paris, France.
Could have seen historic sites and watch naked ladies dance.

Doctor just informed me, I won't be walking for awhile.
I fractured my spine in two places...I could only smile.
You know how I love a good pun, let's make that perfectly clear.
but, breaking my back on Brokeback Mountain, sounds a little queer.

THE BUM

I approach this derelict who's sitting in the street,
an empty bottle of liquor laying at his feet.
If this man doesn't get help soon, he won't stand a chance.
He is so far down and out there's mold growing on his pants.

This guy is filthy dirty I bet he hasn't bathed in weeks,
I don't think I have to tell you how bad this man's body reeks.
I'm glad we're in the open air because I'm seeing something weird,
there are thousands of these tiny little bugs playing in his beard.

There's a hundred bucks in my wallet I know it's not a lot,
to clean and clothe a person but for now it's all I've got.
The bum looks like he is starving, he needs something good to eat.
I think I'll ask him to dinner, get some hamburgers with meat.

I hope that I'm not too late to save this poor man's soul,
I know when you're down and out it really takes its toll.
I rent a cheap hotel room so he can take a hot bath,
I stuff his face with hamburgers and he begins to laugh.

We visit the haberdasher and buy some clothes and shoes,
looking at his smiling face, he no longer has the blues.
He looks so sharp all cleaned up, wearing Eton collars.
I figure this will cost close to 400 dollars.

We go to the barber shop to get his beard erased.
So when he's sleeping in the alley at least he'll be clean faced.
He can stay in the motel for two days to keep out of the cold.
I feel this is so important because he's really pretty old.

I feel rather proud of my sensitivity,
if it weren't for some dumb luck, that bum there could be me.
Knowing I could help this man rally makes me feel glad.
I felt I should do something, after all, he is my dad.

FOOTBALL

I was going to the ballgame at my favorite park.
The day was getting dim but it wasn't really dark.
The team that we were playing was the best team in the league.
Lately we've been playing like we had a case of fatigue.

As this weeks' opponent stepped onto the football field,
they were so darn good I thought my teams' fate was sealed.
I had a season ticket, I knew that we were bad,
although it is not the worst team we have ever had

They have a quarterback whose known as "The Bombardier,"
he always completes the pass if a receiver's near.
When he throws a bullet, it looks just like a tracer,
when he runs the ball, he's as fast as any racer.

I know this may sound heartless but let me make it clear.
I'm hoping a defensive lineman knocks him on his ear.
If they hit him so hard that his pupils dilate,
it might really injure him, wouldn't that be great!

They say that his back-up cannot throw a ball,
in fact his back-up is no darn good at all.
People may think my heart is hard and full of sin,
but I bet a thousand bucks on my team to win.

I WONDER

Gazing out my window at the beautiful sunset,
This has got to be the best that it can possibly get.
I have a question in my mind that I cannot seem to shake,
It's with me when I go to sleep and there when I awake.

Is dusk the end of the day or the beginning of the night?
I thought about it quite a bit and can't figure out what's right.
When the sun dips below the earth, is the day considered done.
I don't know if we can say that just because there is no sun.

Although there is some daylight the night comes creeping in,
I still have to ponder when does night time really begin.
When you think about it, the same can be said about the dawn.
Is it when the day time begins or when night time is gone?

Day-by-day this quandary is messing with my mind,
Is that one of those questions whose answer you can't find?
Maybe I could take some drugs or start pulling out my hair,
Except I finally realize that I don't really care.

THE ALMOST PERFECT COUPLE

My friend was at the altar, his heart was filled with pride.
Staring at the middle door, he waited for his bride.
When the doors were opened up, it really was a sight.
There she stood, a stunning vision, all dressed up in white.

The ceremony that they had, was a beautiful thing.
The vocalist that they hired could really play and sing.
As they left the building, the sun was shining so bright.
The Gods were smiling on them and everything was right.

I said, "This day can't get any better" but they proved me wrong,
The reception was loaded with lots of laughter, booze and song.
They said on the wedding night that the sex was really great,
it wasn't quite a ten but it was better than an eight.

They went to Hawaii for their two week honeymoon.
They said it was beautiful and they would be back soon.
It's been three months now and I've received a thank-you note.
At least that's what I thought it was 'til I read what he wrote.

It was not a thank-you note but a letter about his mate,
He had something to tell me about her and it wasn't great
He told me they decided, now that things have run their course.
They truly hate each other and are filing for divorce.

MY NEW JOB

I was reading all the want ads, searching for a new job.
Looking for a new career that was fitting for old Bob.
I saw one that paid well as an assistant in a lab.
I thought that if I hurried, it's a job that I could grab.

As I walked in, I noticed a man, holding a coffee cup.
He had a strange look in his eyes and his hair was standing up.
He took one look at me and said, "Mr. Ford, you're hired.
You'll be perfect for the job, there are no brains required.

I invented a time machine that will take you into space."
As I hear those final words, all the blood drains from my face.
I'm supposed to save the Earth from a group called Space Raiders.
I start pooping in my pants, and searching for some waders..

I don't need to tell you that I think this man's possessed.
When he straps me to a chair, I feel kind of stressed.
He puts me into a capsule to leave "this island earth."
The pain I'm feeling in my chest, is my heart giving birth.

All the guns and ammo you'll ever need are strewn about.
I've now become so nervous, all my hair is falling out.
I look out the window into what I would call "Deep Space."
There are at least 10 aliens staring me in the face.

I see them start shooting at me, the battle has now begun.
I grab the ammo by the window and shove it in my gun.
I'm killing aliens left and right they're starting to succumb,
I can't believe the hero that I am going to become.

As the door snaps open, I'm sure I've met my eternal rest.
I hear the doctor yell out, "How do you like "Galaxy Quest"
"You mean you put me through this just to test a silly game!"
I feel kind of bad about the person I became.

"That game really scared you good.," I heard him laugh and gloat.
It's at that very moment I grabbed him by the throat.
And as I heard him gasp for air, there was nothing he could do.
"I don't hear any laughing now, I guess the choke's on you."

I FALL IN LOVE

I'm waiting for the fog to lift, it really is quite thick.
I trip over the curb and fall right into this chick.
I accidentally grab her breast as I try to break my fall.
She smacks me hard against my head, she doesn't understand at all

I find out she's the village witch, she even has the hat and broom.
Needless to say when I find this out, I feel a sense of doom.
I apologized profusely for grabbing at her chest.
Now that I look at her, I'm sorry I didn't grab the rest.

I take a chance and ask her out for a nice dinner.
I want her to realize I really am a winner.
There will be no hocus pocus or any kind of trick.
She says that if I try anything she will make me sick.

They say I have the 6th sense on how to make people laugh,
so I start telling her the funniest puns on my behalf.
After she's done laughing, she says she is in love.
Then she puts her arms out and gives me a playful shove.

As I go flying backwards, my feet go flying up,
I accidentally kick her, right in her D cup.
My shoe rips off both her shirt and bra, I feel like a louse.
This wasn't the way I wanted to see what lies beneath her blouse.

THE BATTLE

We were soldiers walking across a dense and grassy field,
all of us were on high alert, keeping our eyes peeled.
The sun was shining brightly as we tried to cross the road.
Some of the men were carrying a really heavy load

We crept up on them silently, the battle had begun.
We had to attack fast, if the battle was to be won.
Colonel Sanders, the chicken, tried to run the other way,
but Cletus, the road warrior, asked all the men to stay.

Although we outnumber the opponents by at least 20 to one,
we knew deep in our hearts, this battle was not already done.
Our scouts come back to tell us our objective is just ahead.
They've all been sunning on the beach and their bodies are all red.

I command all our troops to get back up on their feet,
I want to attack them as soon as they sit down to eat.
Major Sara Lee, now there's a real piece of cake,
she pipes up and tells me that I'm making a big mistake.

The women of the outfit want to attack them when they nap,
I look directly in her eyes and say that's a bunch of crap.
We should attack them now while we're still on the hunt,
not sit back and wait because that's what women want.

A bird on a wire fence suddenly takes flight,
This means that they're moving, soon we will have to fight.
They start spraying us with a poison gas that comes out of a gun,
the best way to avoid this lethal weapon is to turn and run.

Our casualties are heavy, our losses are heavy too.
I try to turn this thing around so we can start anew.
I call for reinforcements but they say they will not come.
Stating they may be stupid, but they certainly aren't dumb.

I wish that I could tell you that we gave it one more try.
Snatching victory from defeat but that would be a lie.
When they started stomping on us, we didn't stand a chance.
They were a family of humans, we an army of ants.

MY GYM TEACHER

Today Jim Locker came to mind, he taught me high school gym.
I really don't remember what made me think of him.
When I was back in high school I wasn't very tall,
in a bunch of students you wouldn't notice me at all.

Mr. Locker taught me sports from gymnastics to football,
no matter what he was teaching he always gave his all.
Another thing that I will say on Mr. Locker's behalf,
he would always play the big buffoon just to make you laugh.

You felt the isolation when you went one on one with him.
No one was able to stop him when he took you to the rim.
If there were any questions about the fairness of the play,
Jim Locker would be out there to make a ruling right away.

That was forty years ago, I wonder how he's been.
I wonder if he's gotten bald with a double chin,
or did he stay hale and hearty and keep himself very fit.
Don't ask me why I think of this, I don't really give a shit

Actually I must admit it would be quite a boon,
if someone would tell me he blew up like a balloon.
So if you know a Jim Locker, please describe him to me.
Better yet, if you have a picture, please send it C.O.D.

THE DANCE CONTEST

They have an old time dance contest in the middle of the town,
I think I'm going to enter it, 'cause I love getting down.
I know when I enroll in it, the people will act all weird.
They all know my dancing nickname, I'm renowned as "Bob the Feared"

I walk into the dancehall in my leisure suit and tie,
I look like John Travolta, a cool looking sort of guy.
Everybody realizes I love to party hardy,
if you want to keep up with me, you better not be tardy.

People will think I have webbed feet the way I dance The Frog.
I'll win all the prizes but I don't want to be a hog.
They all want to see me as I start to dance The Twist.
When I start to make my moves I'm so hard to resist.

Some of the jealous dancers are saying that I am a puss,
the only way I can dance like this is if I am a wuss.
When I do the Salsa whether they like it or not,
everybody in the place has to admit I'm hot.

I'm almost embarrassed when I put on my dancing shoes,
'cause when it comes to contests, I give everyone the blues.
When I start to dancing, every head is spinning,
they all realize they have no chance of winning.

The next song that they are playing, we start to jitterbug,
smoke starts to fill up the room, 'cause I'm burning up the rug.
You could hear the sounds of silence come over the entire hall.
When they come up against me, even the best have to feel small.

As I look across the room, I feel my knees turn to pulp.
The moisture welling up in my throat, makes me have to gulp.
The boogie is the only prize left to win, but I'm not sure I can.
Because walking onto the dance floor is the famous "Boogie Man"

I know I have to beat him, so I've decided what I must do.
So I get some glue and put it on the bottom of his one shoe.
It sounds a little dirty, I think on that we can all agree.
But of course it backfired, 'cause he dances circles around me.

A BAD BREAK

There once was a photographer, a very happy fella,
who liked to sing and dance in the rain, under his umbrella.
He was very busy making lots of folding money,
he felt his life was as good and sweet as any honey.

One day while he was dancing out in the rain,
he slipped on a curb and felt a lot of pain.
As he fell, he heard the snapping of a leg bone,
he called the paramedics on his new cell phone.

They took him to the hospital and put him in a cast.
They said he would be off work, this would not heal real fast.
He asked, "How long will it be?" They said maybe a month or two.
"That will put me out of business if what you say is true."

By the way these words were softly spoken,
you could tell his heart was truly broken.
His friends who came all tried to show him the right way,
so he would realize that he'll dance again someday.

ABOUT MY LAST POEM

This "I'm Pooped" is disgusting, I think I'm going to heave.
That is what my girlfriend said as she packed up to leave.
"I thought you were so sensitive when you wrote about your dogs,
I was hoping you would try to write a poem about my frogs."

She says I should write poems about the moon and my jalopy,
I said, "I'll write one for your frogs if that'll make you hoppy."
She said, "Your story, "A Play on Words" shows what your warped
mind can do,
then you went and made it worse, when you sat down and wrote "Act
2"

The poem, "Lord, Paint me a Rainbow" brought tears to her eyes,
she even liked "Arguing" much to my surprise.
She laughed when she said, the "Vampire" poem would really suck,
the poem about "the Lottery" which talked about my luck.

You started out great with "Maggie" and then "Because I Cared"
when you wrote "Mr. President" It showed you weren't all there.
I will say your poem "Jamie" was a little touching.
and a "A Day to Remember" sent my hands to clutching.

Your poem about "Money" made a lot of sense,
the one "Finding Myself" put me on the fence.
Then you wrote the cute one "Tale of a Knight,"
it makes me think your mind might be alright.

Now you come up with a poem that really turns the bend,
I am telling you right now, this must come to an end.
I'm in love with you so much, but your mind is just not right.
If you keep writing things like this, all we'll do is fight.

Unless you promise not to write poems like this any more,
I'm leaving you forever and she walked right out the door.
Truly I am sorry, I love her so very much,
I'm surely gonna miss her, I hope she stays in touch.

TALE OF A KNIGHT

A knight in shining armor came riding up the hill.
While I stood there watching him, he really took a spill.
As he tumbled downward, he sounded like a ringing bell,
by the time he reached the bottom he really looked like hell.

"Is he looking for a dragon or a damsel in distress?"
the only thing I know is, he really is a nasty mess.
I rush over to him as he lay there on the ground,
he told me he was Sir Gala of the Table Round.

When he was falling down the hill, he went head over heels,
I do not even want to know, the pain that this man feels.
Helping him get back on his feet really was a chore,
between him and his armor, he weighed a ton or more.

So I just got beneath him and gave a mighty push,
he ended up on his feet, I ended on my tush.
As I helped him get up upon his mighty steed,
his armor was soaking wet, I believe he peed.

He said that he was looking for an evil knight,
and if he catches him there's going to be a fight.
My immediate reaction was to laugh out loud of course,
"How you going to fight this man? You can't stay on a horse!"

The evil knight's dragon guards a woman in a tower.
So I'm sure he is going to need every ounce of power.
As I saw him ride away, I was feeling kind of bad,
because I knew all the injuries that Sir Gala had.

Sir Gala has a dirty mind, of that there is no doubt,1
he hopes when he saves this woman, she's going to put out.
To be quite honest with you, I feel the hand's already dealt,
with the way his luck is running, she owns a chastity belt.

THIS JOB IS THE PITS

I go looking for a job in a help wanted ad,
but every time I do it, it just makes me more mad.
Either you have to have an M.B.A. degree.
or they're expecting you to almost work for free.

Today I spotted an ad right in the neighborhood,
I won't have to drive far and the pay is pretty good.
The name of Happy Days Cosmetics doesn't sound too bad.
The only thing they ask for is to be a high school grad.

I get all dressed up in my suit and tie,
they don't ask my age, I'm a happy guy.
The lady interviewing me is as nice as she can be,
she says that she is seriously thinking of hiring me.

She says that I'm hired if I can start right away,
I said I can start right now if that would be okay.
She said she's going to put me in personal inspection,
of course with my dirty mind I'm now getting an erection.

We walk into the back, with two lines of women there,
one line dressed in lab coats and the other almost bare.
I ask her if I'm going to test how their new bra line fits.
She starts to laugh and says to me, "No, you're smelling their armpits."

I'm not sure I hear her right and stare in disbelief.
I don't know how to say it, my heart is filled with grief.
"Did you say you want me to smell all of their armpits?
That is all I'm suppose to do, nothing with their tits?"

I find these women haven't bathed for about a week,
I do not need to tell you how bad these women reek.
She says, "We are testing a new deodorant spray,
just put your nose in her armpit." and I say "No way."

"It's still the best way to test for feminine hygiene."
"I think it's a little weird if you know what I mean."
My dirty mind kicks back in, they make a feminine pad
That definitely involves sex and may not be so bad.

I turn to the lady and say to her, "I quit."
I have to be honest, I just can't handle it.
I do not think I can use my nose looking for a vapor.
I just recalled this company also makes toilet paper.

ANSWER TO ARGUING

My wife and I would argue 'til we couldn't fight no more.
Or one of us would get tired, and walk right out the door.
Some of those fights that we had, were as nasty as nasty gets.
We get along much better now, since we call each other "ex"

I always liked to argue with my dummy of a boss,
when it came to nasty words, I was never at a loss.
Then one fine day he looked at me and he said, "Hey, Bob,
I don't have to take your crap, you no longer have a job."

I admit I often argued even with my friends,
I don't like to argue or the message that it sends.
I feel kind of lonely now, since all my friends have gone away.
There is no one left to argue with and I'm on severance pay.

I guess I'd better look at this horrid life of mine,
if there's a way I could change it, I might feel fine.
And so I did, now I no longer ever argue or fight,
'cause I came to the realization that I AM ALWAYS RIGHT.

BEAR FANS

My son and I are big football fans, we watch it all the time.
We sit back with a bag of chips and a little glass of wine.
I guess when I say fooball, I may be splitting hairs,
'cause the football team we watch is the Chicago Bears.

They are far from the best team in the Northern Hemisphere,
I'm not sure what it says about us, we still sit and cheer.
Every year we think that the Bears are going to take it all.
After watching a few games, we bang our heads against the wall.

We then start to contemplate why the team is so darn bad,
by telling ourselves about all the injuries we've had.
Our front line is hurting and the QB's in a cast,
because of all these problems the team is fading fast.

I keep watching with my son, we're out of the playoff games,
another season we waited for has gone down in flames.
They put in the rookies and the crippled, fresh from their steam bath,
All of a sudden, once again, they have led us down the path.

Maybe it's next year that is going to be our year,
I find it kind of odd, that's what Cub fans always hear.
"You don't have to watch the Bears!" that is what they say,
but if we don't watch them, we'd have to watch Green Bay.

Wasting another afternoon just seems to be so wrong,
when we could have fun playing a lively game of Ping-Pong.
I'm sure you did not read this just to hear me whine,
to show you I'm a good guy, I'm going to end this rhyme.

NATURE

Sitting here, looking up at all the trees,
leaves blowing gently in the summer breeze.
The lovely lawn that looks so emerald green,
it's the prettiest thing you have ever seen.

Touched by the beauty of the clouds up in the sky,
I feel a little moisture filling in my eye.
Taking in a deep breath of the fresh summer air,
my mind is so happy, it is without a care.

Walking toward the gorgeous blooming flower bed,
visions of color start dancing in my head.
So I guess what most people say is definitely true,
It really is amazing what Mother Nature can do.

It's sad to think that soon the leaves will be falling down,
all their Autumn colors will be laying on the ground.
That means pretty soon I will be out there with a rake,
Working my poor butt off, unable to take a break.

Thinking of another thing that makes me bust my ass,
when that lovely lawn grows, I have got to mow the grass.
When I take in a deep breath and I start to sneeze,
I am reminded of my different allergies.

Those beautiful white clouds darken and it begins to pour,
I notice streams of water coming out my basement door.
I get down on my knees so the garden can be weeded,
another little task, just exactly what I needed.

Mother Nature meant a lot to me when I was just a lad.
It seems the more I know of her now, the more I feel bad.
I know this may sound really awful, like I'm some kind of jerk,
all Mother Nature means to me now, is a ton of extra work.

FLIGHT OF FANCY

I'm called the aviator because I often fly my plane,
I do it so frequently people say that I'm insane.
I first started out flying a couple hours a day,
It would help me to relax is all that I can say.

Flying made those headaches of mine finally disappear,
without my pain inside my head, my mind became quite clear.
Three years ago I was flying late into the afternoon,
but every time I would land the plane I feel like it's too soon.

My stomach acid problem at last came to an end.
This sea inside me has calmed down, flying is my friend.
I don't want my airplane to ever touch the ground again,
when I fly it sideways I'm put into the world of Zen.

This year I'm trying something no matter how much I pay,
soon I will be flying twenty-four hours in a day.
Yes, if everything goes exactly the way I have it planned,
I'll soon be getting even closer to finding neverland.

THE KUMQUAT INCIDENT

I'm telling of this incident that caused a little flap,
so you'll watch where you're going and not fall into the trap.
This story happened to me a year or so ago,
and none of this is my fault, I just want you to know.

I went into the grocery store looking for a kumquat,
I wanted to taste one to see if I liked it or not.
The color's orange or yellow, I can't tell I'm color blind.
the pulp is awfully sour but I kind of like the rind.

Looking at this silly fruit, I trip over a rubber ball,
The fruit flies out of my hand and bounces wildly off the wall.
The manager makes an entrance and it hits him in the head,
because of this untimely mishap he almost ends up dead.

How he can blame this thing on me really is a hoot,
saying that I almost killed him with my tiny fruit.
"Sir," I said, "to hurt you was not really my desire."
He looked me in the eyes and called me a fat liar.

He says he's going to sue me for everything I've got,
I tell him, "Go ahead, I haven't got a whole lot."
The security guards grab me and throw me out the door.
They say that I am not welcome in this store anymore.

They have now set up a special coalition,
a guard at every door, preventing my admission.
It becomes a challenge to get by all these guys,
what I have to do is come up with a disguise.

I won't say what the disguise is, I can't give it away.
But I went shopping there this morning, that is all I'll say.
To give you just a little hint, I can tell you how it feels.
to do all your grocery shopping in a pair of 3 inch heels.

SEARCH FOR A FOUNTAIN

I'm going on a journey to find the fountain of youth,
Because I was just told, I am getting long in the tooth.
My dentist said my roots go deep into my jaw,
they are in so deep, they should be against the law.

I said they are so long because I am older than dirt.
All the hairs I have are gray, even those beneath my shirt.
Every time I rise from a chair, I make a little sound.
It annoys some people, at least that is what I have found.

I have arthritis in my back, also in both my hands.
If I'm going to find that fountain, I need to make some plans.
I need to write it down now, before it slips my mind
People say I am forgetful, but that's a bit unkind.

My eyesight is so bad I can't even see fifty feet.
I'd probably miss the fountain if it was across the street.
My knee hurts so much that if I don't wear my brace,
It is very difficult to get from place to place.

To find this missing fountain, I should buy a book.
Maybe it would tell me where I can go and look
I guess I'll just have to sit here and wear a silly little smile,
because to discover the fountain of youth, may take me quite a while

WORDS OF WISDOM

A little boy came up to me and says, "Your hair is very gray,
and as I look at you, I see you weren't born yesterday.
I have a couple questions, I need the answer real soon.
Why are aliens green and is there a man up in the moon?

I need answers for a science test that I take today."
"Of course I know the answers son." What else was I to say?
"You never see a life force when the satellite goes by,
there is a good reason for this and I will tell you why.

I think you will find my reasoning is really very sound.
It's because all the aliens like to live under the ground
So aliens aren't really green if the truth be told,
since they're always underground they're covered with a mold.

Look up in the evening sky, when the moon is shining bright,
if you look very closely, you'll understand that I am right.
You will see the moon has a mouth, a nose and yes, two eyes.
When I say there's a man in there, it should be no surprise.

There is a man inside the moon, you should listen to me son,
I can even give you his name, he's known as Jackie Gleason.
Although they may be moldy, aliens may appear to be green.
Have a look at Alf on t.v., to know exactly what I mean."

I turned to the lady next to me, who at that time was my wife.
I said, "I am watching too much t.v., I've got to get a life.
The little boy turned away as happy as can be.
"Thank you for the wisdom you just passed on to me."

I guess that foolish little boy took me at my word,
they have him in an asylum now, that is what I heard.
He's known as "Mr. President" and as far as I can tell.
So he is locked very securely in a little padded cell.

Serious

A SAD DAY IN THE NEIGHBORHOOD

I heard some sad news today,
Mr. Rodgers passed away.
A man whose heart was good and pure,
and full of love that is for sure.

When he took off his coat and put on his sweater,
He made billions of kids feel a whole lot better.
when his show finally came to an end,
they all felt that they lost their best friend.

He taught them ethics and how they should play,
He will be missed is all that I can say.
I know he'd want us to be happy, and I know I should,
but today's not a beautiful day in the neighborhood.

LORD, PAINT ME A RAINBOW

Lord, paint me a rainbow with your magic brush,
I'm in no hurry, so there's no need to rush.
How big do I want it? I don't really care,
make it the whole sky, or from just here to there.

Lord, paint me a rainbow of red, blue, yellow and green,
it will help to remind me I should never be mean.
Lord, paint me a rainbow of blue, yellow, green and red,
so I know things will be better if I just use my head.

Lord, paint me a rainbow of green, yellow, red and blue,
to remind me to love everyone, especially You.
Lord, paint me a rainbow of red, blue, green and yellow,
so I'll always try to be a kind and helpful fellow.

Lord, paint me a rainbow of just silver and gold,
just because it sounds pretty and I'm getting old.
Thanks for putting them up in the sky so I can see,
the kind of a person you really want me to be.

HAPPY FATHER'S DAY, DAD

Father's Day is coming and I am feeling kind of sad,
because I don't remember a whole lot about my dad.
I may not have a lot of them, but let me make things clear,
the memories I do have of him, I hold very dear.

I remember when we'd play some sports out in the backyard.
We would toss a ball back and forth, sometimes pretty hard.
We played in the yard so often, we wore dirt holes in the grass,
because we'd be playing baseball or I'd go out for a pass.

The one memory that I have that keeps running through my head,
is that my dad was really nice and kept his family fed.
Or the day he came home and took his smokes out from where he had
them hid.
He said, "I'm going to quit smoking." and you know by God he did.

Since he was young my dad's hair was gray, and please excuse the pun,
but it's this hair raising trait he passed on to his only son.
I got his sense of humor, the kind that makes you slap your knee.
But since I don't get to many laughs, I guess the joke's on me.

Dad, if you are listening to me, in heaven up above,
please know that I still think of you, and send you all my love.
I wrote this poem to let you know what a good job you had done.
And to thank you for all your love, I'm signing it, Bob, your son.

TO JAMIE

I remember a little girl of three,
who knew exactly what she wanted to be.
When asked what it was, she had the answer,
"I'm going to be a talented dancer."

By five or six, she began to learn form,
as she and her classmates tapped up a storm.
She made some mistakes, I guess one or two,
but she was a kid, so what else was new.

By the time she reached the age of nine or ten
I went back to watch her dancing once again
It's amazing to see how much she improves
she has learned all the steps and all of the moves.

When she was twelve or thirteen, she began to teach,
an incredible goal for a young girl to reach.
This time she dances up on her toes,
her and her class are looking like pros.

I saw that little girl dance again yesterday,
let me tell you what I saw just blew me away.
The dances she did with a bright smile on her face,
were done with a beautiful style, rhythm, and grace.

So as I end this poem and get up to go,
there is one thing that I think you should know.
It's like watching a seedling grow into a tree.
Jamie, you grew into what you wanted to be.

FINDING MYSELF

I will try to find myself today,
I'll look up, down, and every which way.
I don't know what I'm going to find,
I hope the answer can ease my mind.

I'll look from without, I'll look from within,
and try to find out what my life has been.
I'll look to my left, then I'll look to my right,
to see if I can find some kind of insight.

I'll try to look high, and I'll try to look low,
try to find answers I don't really know.
I'm going to look around for some kind of clue,
whether it be false or whether it be true.

I must try to learn from my many lifetime mistakes,
and work to correct them no matter how long it takes.
I wonder should I go through all this extra work,
when it might turn out that I am just a big jerk.

I might just be playing some tricks on my mind,
who knows what kind of person I'm going to find.
I'd better quit searching before I get into a jam,
And find out I'm not quite as perfect as I think I am.

No, I'll keep looking, I don't mind,
the answers are so hard to find.
Who am I kidding, I know where I should start.
If you need to find answers, look into your heart.

A DAY TO REMEMBER

Watching the news on the 11th of September,
turned out to be something I will always remember.
The 1st plane had crashed and the sky had turned gray,
how tragic for some, was all I could say.

After watching this happen, my heart became numb,
not knowing that this attack had only begun.
As the buildings fell down I started to cry,
'cause thousands of people were going to die.

Thousands of kids would be without Mom or Dad,
and the feelings inside me were nothing but sad.
I thought of all of the firefighters and many a cop,
as they all lost their lives trying to give help at the top.

Who in the world would be capable of such acts?
Tell me some of their names and give me some facts!
My heart filled with anger, then went to hate.
Bomb them right now, I do not want to wait.

I said a little prayer and ended with Amen,
and told myself I do not what to be like them.
They want us to separate and hate each other, that is what they planned.
But if we go ahead and do it brother, we give them the upper hand.

Let's rid the world of racial profiling, prejudice and hate,
and stand together side by side that will really make us great!
I want to mention something to those of us who still remain.
Get back to your normal life, so those who died, didn't die in vain.

Let us say a prayer for those who died,
and say a prayer for those who survived.
Let us say a prayer for their family and friends,
finally say a prayer for all Americans.
GOD BLESS AMERICA!!

DEATH OF A POET

I've been lying in this hospital bed for about a week,
waiting for the final eternal peace everyone must seek.
I hear a noise out in the hall, it's getting hard to breathe,
the Angel of Death just walked in, he says that we must leave.

The saddest thing about this is, as I'm about to die,
no one is around me, so there will be no last goodbye.
First I want to apologize to anyone that I hurt,
before they come to take me away and put me in the dirt.

The trait I got from granny was to try and please everyone,
I am telling you right now my friends, it simply can't be done.
When it came to getting that trait, I wish I could have fought her.
I pray to God I didn't pass it on to my son or daughter.

There are many things in my life that I am sorry for,
and if I lived longer there would probably be some more.
It's funny when your time here on earth finally is through,
you might want to correct mistakes, but there's nothing you can do.

I wish I would have gone to school or maybe learned a trade,
that may be the biggest mistake I have ever made.
I would have earned a paycheck that would have paid all my bills.
not having enough money was the cause of all my ills.

There is one thing that I can say, on my own behalf,
I was always pretty good at making people laugh.
The other thing that always made me feel higher than a kite,
was the kick that I would get, reading poems that I would write.

Whether it's to hell or heaven that I'm supposed to go,
I feel there is just one more thing, I want you to know.
If I get to heaven and the Lord gives me a seat,
the dogs and I will wait there till once again we meet.

But if I end up in Hell, I will try to use my clout.
I'll tell the devil all my puns until he throws me out.
The Angel of Death says I must put an end to all of this,
so good-bye, I love you all and I seal it with a kiss.

WHAT IF...

As I sit here in my truck, I drift back to my teens,
I'm thinking how I could have been a man of means.
When I graduated high school, I studied dentistry
I probably would have made it too, except I flunked chemistry.

Is your destiny already planned or do you have a voice?
Or is it a little bit of both? That would be my choice.
It's affected by all the decisions that you make each day,
but also by the circumstances that often come your way.

Be careful what you wish for is how the saying goes,
' cause what happens when you get that wish, no one really knows.
If only one thing in my life was somehow redirected,
how not only my life, but other lives would be affected.

Let's just say I did not fail and a dentist I became,
There'd be no money problems with D.D.S. after my name.
I'd be living in the suburbs in a large estate,
probably have a new car too, wouldn't that be great!

My kids would both be happy and so would my ex-wife,
I think this is wonderful, I have a different life.
Then just like a lighting bolt it comes crashing down on me.
I said it would be different, but how different would it be.

Then I got to thinking what changes would be done,
I probably would have had a different wife for one.
Because of that, Brian and Kelly would no longer be,
of course those would be changes number two and number three.

My experiences wouldn't be the same, neither would my friends.
The more I got to think about it, the list just never ends.
Thinking about your new life can also make you sad,
since you don't know for certain, it might be twice as bad.

Be careful what you wish for, a genie might appear,
and if he grants your wish, you might lose all that you hold dear.
I thought if these things occurred would I like them or not.
I leaned back, closed my eyes, and thanked God for what I got.

A CHANGE

I took a walk along the beach, a twinkle in my eye.
It turned out to be a big, bright star in the evening sky.
Although it was not the first star I saw on this clear night,
I made a wish upon it, though I knew it wasn't right.

As I went a little further I heard a waterfall,
When I came up next to it, it looked like a liquid wall.
It was a lovely feeling as the mist fell upon this place.
Like a soft, silken cloth that is gently run across your face.

The fresh scent that surrounded it was something to behold.
It took me back to my youth, I didn't feel quite so old.
As I turned to leave this place I felt my toes squish in the sand.
I realize that my life did not turn out exactly as I planned.

I can't believe the inspiration I found on that night.
I decided that little things will help to make things right.
Now my heart is filled with wonder and has grown a pair of wings,
and they start to flutter every time I hear the song a birdie sings.

TO ERIC

Eric, I heard you are going to Iraq.
Well, keep your head low and an eye on your back.
You're going to be living at the edge of hell,
and we want you to come back here, alive and well.

There will be voices that are a little unkind,
who will say to your face that you've lost your mind.
When I heard you re-upped I felt just like a swine.
'cause one of those voices is going to be mine.

I was going to ask you, what were you thinking,
or better yet, what the hell were you drinking?
Now if you are hungry you must beware,
and not overeat the sand which is there.

Your friends here at Wal-Mart all want you to know,
we were sad when we found out where you had to go.
Of course there are worse things than this Iraqi War crap,
You could be forced to listen to some of Chris's new rap.

If you decide not to go, I've got it all planned,
I can take the paint hammer and smash up your hand.
We'll break all your fingers, each and every last one,
I know they won't take you if you can't hold a gun.

Take care of yourself Eric, all kidding aside,
what ever happens there try to take it in stride.
Here's something else I know is going to bring you good cheer,
you won't have to hear any of my jokes for over a year.

Pets

MY KITTY

I have a little kitty cat that loves to play with mice,
the only trouble is, she doesn't always play so nice.
She grabs them by the tail and bats them like a little ball,
then she has to chase them halfway down the hall.

I heard a strange noise in the kitchen just the other night,
it was such an awful racket that it gave me quite a fright.
I went downstairs and slowly opened up the kitchen door,
I could not believe what I saw sitting on the kitchen floor.

There was my little kitty and her mice friends on their knees,
all their tails a-wagging as they gnaw on a piece of cheese.
When they are done eating and lie down to take their naps,
I'm going to have to go out and buy many no kill traps.

It seems my little kitty won't chase the mice out of my house,
I suppose I should be upset but I'm not going to grouse.
Because when it comes right down to it and push comes to shove.
The one thing my cat's good for is unconditional love.

BUTTERCUP

I once had a kitty, a black, brown and white Calico.
A little over three years now I had to let her go.
She was pretty as a flower so I named her Buttercup,
I gave her to my ex-girlfriend the night that we broke up.

That cat knew how to handle me and play me for a sap.
Soon as I sat down in a chair, she'd jump onto my lap.
She would just look up at me till I petted her colorful fur.
Before you knew it, she'd be on her back and begin to purr.

Now you know how this cat played me like a fiddle,
answer for me if you can this simple little riddle.
When I came back from the kitchen carrying a load of treats,
can you take one wild guess who got to join in on the eats?

GOODBYE, MAGGIE

Thank you for bringing years of joy,
to both our little girl and boy.
You could hold two tennis balls in your mouth like falling off a log,
and catch a Frisbee also, you were quite a wonderful dog.

Remembering your happy tail and sweet little face,
means that you'll surely be missed and so hard to replace.
As far as we're concerned, you were as sweet as candy.
We hope your in heaven now, outside playing with Mandy.

You always considered everyone your friend,
and you stayed that way right up to the very end.
We all remember your beautiful coat with the color of light gold.
How you acted like a puppy, even though you were seven years old.

So remember us with lots of love,
and watch over us from up above.
And if there is one thing that makes our spirits soar,
is knowing that you are not hurting anymore.

As I finish up this loving poem,
we hope you're happy in your new home.
We all want you to know, even though we had to part,
Maggie, you will be remembered forever in our heart.

BECAUSE I CARED

Whenever I put a pet to sleep, it seemed I lost a friend,
and I thought that the pain I felt was never going to end.
When I took them to the vet and knew we were going to part,
the sadness and the guilt that I would feel, filled my aching heart.

Did I do the right thing? Should I have let them live?
Did I cover all the bases, give all that I could give?
Then one night I dreamt about a Rainbow bridge, all my pets were there,
playing together and running about, they didn't have a care.

They told me that their love for me always will remain.
Because I loved them enough to go and ease their pain.
Now they all are happy and say they are feeling mighty fine.
Also they are thanking me for putting their needs before mine.

When their time on Earth is getting short and it starts to bring you to tears.
Remember all the joys and memories they gave you throughout the years.
And when their pain is more than you feel they should bear,
make sure you do what's right, to show them that you care.

GOODBYE, ABBY

Little did I know what a great friend I was going to meet,
when I stopped you and your buddy from running near the busy street.
You were a young black Lab, he was a different type of pup.
When you came for the dog biscuit, I quickly snatched you up.

I looked down the street to see if someone was coming after you.
When I didn't see anyone, there was only one thing left to do.
I put you in the front seat of my milk truck so I could use the phone.
Mom and Ahma said to bring you with me so you wouldn't be alone.

I hate to admit this fact because I felt like such a schmuck,
by the time I got off the phone, you ate every Milk-Bone on the truck.
We put an ad in the paper and when no one staked a claim,
the family got together and made Abigail your name.

Everyone who knew you, remembers your happy, wagging tail.
Whenever you would meet someone, it would start going without fail.
I won't say you wagged it fast but if you just had bare knees,
when it started going you could actually feel a breeze.

When Melissa brought her dog Cassie to live with us, she caused you lots of strife.
But looking back on it in reality she added years on to your life.
When you got older, you may have heard us snicker at your face.
with your velvet black coat, your white beard and eyebrows looked so out of place.

We didn't want to let you go but we felt it was a must.
as long as you were living here, you gave to us your trust.
We felt a little comfort as we walked out the vet's front door.
Knowing deep down in our hearts you were not hurting anymore.

Brandy misses you a lot, sometimes she's sleeping in your bed.
I know that you are listening, by the way you tilt your head.
Thank you for giving us all the memories and love,
these are both things that we could never get enough of.

I'm sure by now you're at Rainbow's Bridge with Maggie and Mandy.
I picture you three playing together happy as can be.
I want you ladies to be good and look for us every now and then.
I don't know how long it's going to be but we will meet again.

FAREWELL TO BRANDY

Brandy, you will always be remembered as our little girl.
When it came to dogs you were considered quite a pearl.
Your sweet face and golden hair soft as any cotton,
cannot be replaced and will not be soon forgotten.

We first got you when I was out there selling meat,
your owner didn't want you and placed you at my feet.
I called Mom and she said that I should bring you home,
now that you have left us I need to write this poem.

I came into the house with a tiny ball of fur,
as soon as Mom saw you she knew you belonged to her.
Through your life with us, you and her became best of friends,
even though you had to leave that friendship never ends.

We sometimes had to laugh when you used the couch to wipe your face.
We should have gotten real mad at you but that was not the case.
When you laid down on your side and started pawing at the rug,
we always felt like bending down and giving you a big hug.

You would go into the toy box and pick the biggest one,
and tossed it all around like it brought you so much fun.
When you see the other dogs, too many here to list,
tell them that we love them and just how much they are missed.

It really is no wonder why we thought you were a prize,
it looked like you had eyeliner around both of your eyes.
These are the kind of things that are so hard to forget.
I'm sure there will be many more we haven't thought of yet.

We didn't want to put you down but it became a must,
you were in such awful pain and you gave to us your trust.
So go and play with the family dogs, but when you guys are though
think of Bruno, your friend down here, cause he also misses you.

MY TWO FURRY FRIENDS

Abby and Brandy are our dogs at home.
They are the reason that I wrote this poem.
Abby a Black Lab, at 14, is old I suppose.
How much time we have left together, God only knows.

Brandy is a small dog that is 9 years old,
she's pretty feisty, I would even say bold.
They're quite a combo, but on their behalf,
they're easy to love 'cause they make us laugh.

Abby's white face and nose show her old age,
so does my white hair, it must be the rage.
Brandy's been a barker since she was a pup.
You can yell all you want, she just won't shut up

If we just feed them and make sure they're okay,
they're happy as sin for the rest of the day.
For all of their love, I'm deeply indebted,
'cause all that they ask is just to be petted.

If I feel bad, I open the door and I'm sure,
that my two furry friends have found the perfect cure.
'Cause when I open that door, all trouble I have pales,
Abby and Brandy smile at me, by wagging their tails.

BYE CRU'

What do you remember when you think of Cru'?
We thought of a number of things, here are just a few.
Whenever Mom would go outside, she knew when the phone was ringing,
because whenever it would start to ring, Cru' would start his singing.

Mom will always remember, as you sat beside her bed,
How you would like to look at her, till she'd pat you on the head.
She'd say "Good Night" and give a kiss to her favorite pup,
then pick up your blanket and cover you all up.

Whenever you came up to Cru', it was easy to love him without fail.
You couldn't help but love that big Doberman, with his tiny tail.
The vet had cut his tail too short, but Cru' did not seem to care.
It made it easier when he backed up, to sit upon a chair.

You always whined to get your way, and I don't mean to mock,
but you really looked quite silly, always carrying Mom's sock.
The friends you left behind here when you had to go,
were Mia, Nadia, and don't forget Shadow.

We're very sad you left us, but we know you're with the best,
Maggie, Lacy, and Tucker, not to mention all the rest.
We know that you are all watching over us from heaven up above.
Know that we remember everyone of you and send you all our love.

BONNIE THE SCOTTIE

My parents always had a thing for Scotties,
not for Goldens, Spaniels or even Rotties.
They had the same thing when it came to a name,
They'd name her Bonnie, it was always the same.

Now that this Bonnie has passed, please don't think I'm screwy,
she'll be remembered most, as a dog with a chewie.
It was her favorite thing that can not be denied,
'cause it seemed like there was always one by her side.

When you took Bonnie out for a walk, she thought it was her show.
She'd go when you wanted to stop, and stop when you wanted to go.
My sister Joan said the one she knew for sure,
was that taking out Bonnie was an adventure.

When the hot Phoenix sun shone in the house, she had to protect herself.
So she would lie under the table, or hide on the bottom bookshelf.
Mom would take a cold drink out to her lounge chair,
she'd look down at her feet, and Bonnie would be there.

They found Cancer in her paw, and a liver that was failing,
Mom soon realized that poor Bonnie must surely be ailing.
She knew that putting her down would make her weep,
Mom made a promise she knew she had to keep.

The one pet owners make to take care of their pet,
Bonnie says "thank you," she's forever in your debt.
Mom, if you could see Bonnie, you wouldn't be sad,
She's with all the other Bonnies and of course, Dad.

Baby

CHERYL

My name is Cheryl or so they say,
I guess that I'm coming out today,
It's Feb. 18th, the hour I don't know,
But now is the time I'm supposed to show.

Hey! It's awfully cold out in this air
I wish I could climb back inside there,
That man in the white outfit has raised his hand
and a slap on my fanny he's going to land.

Who's that woman? It must be my new mother.
I'm glad I got her instead of another.
She looks nice as nice can be,
I'll bet she'll take good care of me.

They're pouring a liquid from a cup,
I guess they want to clean me up.
They're preparing me for father dear,
For the first time he will appear.

I think I hear him coming now,
Could that be him? Holy Cow!
He looks like a smart, handsome lad,
Oh, darn it all that's not my dad.

I hope my father looks like him
I think I see him coming in.
Is this my father that I must choose?
Well, I guess some you win, some you lose.

You know which part is the real sin?
Most people say I look just like him
Well, in about another week,
At my new home, I'll get to peek.

I go home today with Mom and Dad.
I must admit that I am glad.
I love them both they're very dear,
I know that I'll be happy here.

TIMOTHY HICKEY

I'm sitting here in this peaceful place,
Where the clouds brush up against my face;
I have to stay here, it is believed,
Until the moment that I'm conceived.

My body is starting to feel light,
I wonder if this could be my big night.
This feeling to me is quite endearing,
My present form is now disappearing.

Now I am inside my mother's womb,
For a nine months wait, I must assume.
And, if my assumption is proven true,
Feb. 18th is when I will be due.

While in here I can feel myself growing,
Now all my features and limbs are showing.
I'm fully grown, I'm big and strong.
When I come out, I won't take long.

So let the banners now be unfurled,
I've make my entrance into the world.
This world down here is mighty bright,
I an hardly see with all this light.

Looking around this brand new place,
I see this friendly smiling face.
That must be my mom, she sure looks nice,
I'll bet she hasn't a single vice.

Pretty soon I'll see my new dad, Leo is his name,
making me a happy child, I'm sure will be his aim.
And one thing that I want to make absolutely clear,
is my mom and dad to me, are very, very dear.

I know my parents hope as I face each and every test,
That I throw back both my shoulders and do my very best.
But I will assure them that won't be at all tricky,
I'll be proud to be known as Timothy Paul Hickey.

DANIEL JASON

I'm up here in the sky so high
Watching the earth as it goes by,
To be born is the thing I yearn
I guess I'll have to wait my turn.

My soul has a feeling it has never had before
It's a wonderful feeling-one I really adore,
I feel so happy, I am truly relieved
Cause they say you feel like this when you're conceived.

I've come down to earth on a blanket of air
And landed in this spot but not without care,
I am scared of the dark, but I will try to be brave
I'm supposed to spend nine months in what looks like a cave.

I'm making my entrance into this brand new world
Where to me many things will soon be unfurled.
As I'm cut from my mother and brought to her side
I see both of my parents are beaming with pride.

They look very nice and I'm very glad,
That they're going to be my mom and my dad.
As for my father he is a real weird son-of-a-gun,
He keeps hitting the doctor saying "That's my son, that's my son!"

It's not nice to say this I suppose
But my dad has a very large nose,
He turned his head but didn't mean any harm
He broke two doctor's legs and one nurse's arm.

As for my mother, she no longer looks fat.
I guess 'cause I vacated the spot I was at.
I'll go home in a few days and I'm sure that I'll find,
a place where I'm loved and all the people are kind.

My sister Debbie, who's a cute little miss,
came up and game me a big hug and a kiss.
I bought her a toy I'm hoping she will enjoy,
and won't mind the intrusion of a new baby boy.

When it came to picking my parents I didn't have a choice
But they would be the ones I'd have asked for if I had a voice,
As mom washes me up in my little basin,
I know I will be happy as Daniel Jason.

AVA JOAN PAUL

I'm waiting here in heaven and I'm trying to be calm,
I'm kind of antsy for someone to be my Dad and Mom.
Wait! I'm getting this great feeling and I do believe,
A lovely young couple is now going to receive.

I've been in here for 9 months now, I think that I'll come out.
I can't wait any longer, so I'm taking the short route.
They think it's going to take me many hours to arrive,
but I'm going to surprise them and come out in less than five.

As I pop my head out, I see a flashing device,
My Dad is taking pictures, I hope my hair looks nice.
When it comes to hair my Mom is a bit of a nut,
and if it's not quite right, she will give it a quick cut.

As I look at these two people, my brand new Mom and Dad,
my Mom is really pretty, and my Dad is not half bad.
Both of them are so sweet, I'm as happy as can be.
I know that they'll do their best to take good care of me.

I met most of my relatives from both sides of the clan,
it seems like every one wants to be my biggest fan.
I heard them say my name, it sounds like sweet cologne.
I know that I will be happy here with the name of Ava Joan.

KAITLIN BREE FORD

It was 5:30 Sunday morn when I suddenly awoke,
I found out later on, that was the moment Mom's water broke.
Even though my water was gone, I felt I was doing fine,
but after 20 hours of labor it's time to draw the line.

I decide to give a push so I could stick my head out,
my folks were so glad to see me of that there is no doubt.
When I slid out and saw my Pop, I thought, "What a handsome lad,"
Then I turned around and saw my Mom, she's cuter than my Dad.

It's been two days since I've arrived and I've met most of 'the crew,'
but there are so many of them that I'm not sure who is who.
When my grandparents met me, of course, they went completely wild.
The reason they're so happy to see me? I'm their first grandchild.

The rest of my new relatives seem as nice as they can be.
They all really seem to care and want to show their love for me.
I know living down here is going to bring a little strife,
but with every one behind me, I'm sure I'll have a great life.

From the looks of the females in this family I've seen,
I'm sure to have inherited some of their beauty gene.
Then my parents gave me something that's as beautiful as me,
they came up with and gave me the lovely name of Kaitlin Bree.

CHRISTOPHER DANIEL ZANDER

I'm sitting here on a fluffy cloud, looking down on Earth.
In just a short 9 months from now my Mom will give me birth
I am supposed to come out on the 15th of July,
I don't like to be late so on the date you can rely.

I start heading from the sky to my Mommy's womb.
When I get in there it is like a small dark room.
I know it's just a short time this is going to last,
but when it is time to leave, I'll get out real fast

The 9 months are now over, and it's my time to appear.
Pretty soon I'll see my parents who I will hold so dear.
Wow, I finally see my Mom she is really pretty,
my Dad doesn't look as good but I hear he's witty

All my relatives seem as nice as they can be.
They come into the room, and gush all over me.
They pick me up, give me a hug and a little kiss
I figured out my name, because they all call me Chris.

I know that I'm going to love both of my new folks.
Even though they have a friend who tells really bad jokes
That is what Mommy gets for working at Wal-Mart,
she knew she'd meet some people who weren't very smart.

I know that I will be loved by everyone I know,
and deep inside my heart I can feel a certain glow.
If you haven't seen me yet, better come and take a gander,
because I am a handsome lad named Christopher Daniel Zander

Holiday

ALIEN KIDNAPPING

I'm kidnapped by aliens and taken to their UFO.
They say they want to question me on just how much I know.
Saying that people from Planet Earth all seem pretty dumb,
they're giving me a test to see if I know where they come from.

We're going to the Cosmic Bar on the dark side of the Moon,
at the rate of speed we're going, we should arrive there pretty soon.
They put me on a barstool and say let the test commence,
I'm not the brightest bulb in the box and I feel tense.

They send out the first two aliens that look like candy bars.
I yell out, "I'm not naive, they're from the planet they call Mars."
Out walk two stunning blondes that get a rise out of my penis,
this one's so very simple, they both have to be from Venus.

The next ETs, wearing rings, sit down and swivel left to right.
My captors tell me to take a guess, they haven't got all night.
I feel it is their respect that I have to earn,
so I say quite calmly, "They're probably from Saturn"

The next group makes some comments, more than most people can
endure,
I've seen these aliens long enough, of my answer now I'm sure.
Beings that act like that, seem to have made their planet famous,
because they are perfect assholes they must be from Uranus.

The alien with the smoking flesh, looks so very hot,
he has to be from Mercury, more likely than not.
The one that is full of gas, cobalt blue and saying brrr,
can only come from the fifth planet, the one called Jupiter

The guy who looks like Mickey Mouse's pet, who has a floppy ear,
can only be from the Planet Pluto that is very clear.
At this alien guessing game, I've become quite deft,
the final guy is from Neptune, the only planet left.

Every one applauds, then the room begins to shake.
I hear someone saying, "Hey Dad, are you awake?"
Hurry up, get off the couch and put some shoes on your feet.
You're supposed to take us out for a night of trick or treat.

THE PERFECT PRESENT

As I start my Christmas shopping, I am looking at my list.
I'm checking it twice to see if there is anyone I missed.
Now that I am unattached I have to go to the store,
I can't depend on someone to shop for me anymore.

I foresee a problem brewing if I go out to shop.
I have no idea what to get or where I should stop.
Where do you go to find everyone the perfect Christmas gift?
I don't what to buy something that will get somebody miffed.

Is shopping really indigenous only to the female gender?
Or is it just as good for a male who likes to be a spender?
What kind of gift do you get for your son and his lovely wife?
Something they will enjoy for the rest of their natural life.

I see the big K-Mart symbol at a local store,
another has Wal-Mart in big letters by the door.
Should I go to Kohl's, all these stores make my poor head spin.
I'm thinking my daughter and her spouse don't want a popcorn tin.

Scarcely have I ever picked a good gift for anyone I knew,
when it comes to giving gifts I guess I haven't got a clue.
This is going to be the year I will turn it all around,
let me tell you about the answer that I think I found.

Periodically I come up with a doozie of a thought,
the perfect present for everyone is what I went out and bought.
I do not have to worry about shopping anymore,
I'm giving everyone a gift card from their favorite store.

THE MAN IN THE RED SUIT

I know a man that I see only once a year.
But everyone I know of holds him very dear.
He's always wearing saucy clothes and his favorite color is red.
That's the color on his pants, his coat and the cap that's on his head.

I guess that you would have to say he is pretty wide.
I'm not talking up and down, I'm talking side to side.
When I see him once a year, he is never any thinner,
but I think we can all agree he really is a winner.

He dresses kind of funny, but I don't mean to imply,
that this good friend of mine is not a regular guy.
I hear he tends to go up north when he leaves from here.
He likes to sit his butt down and have a steak and beer.

He has such long snowy white hair and the perfect furry beard.
When you take one look at him, you're immediately endeared.
He never wears any shoes, he prefers a certain kind of boot.
Always buying gifts for everyone, he must have a lot of loot.

He's involved more with little children, loves them with all his heart.
I think if he had his way, he'd take them all out to Wal-Mart.
I hear that he owns reindeer and when he's up north they say,
he likes to hitch them up in winter and let them pull his sleigh.

So if you see him in your house carrying a big sack,
be sure to leave milk and cookies, he loves a little snack.
Leave carrots for the reindeer, for strength to fly away,
that way you can be sure they come back every Christmas Day.

HAPPY THANKSGIVING

The Thanksgiving holiday to me is always such a treat,
it's the only holiday I know, where all you do is eat.
You do not have to sing a song or give any one a gift,
the only thing you have to do is find a knife and fork to lift.

You don't have to wait for midnight before you can have some fun.
You don't have to sit around 'til all the fireworks are done.
They cook up a turkey with dressing and all that other stuff.
When it comes to making turkey dinner they can't make enough.

I really have a taste for some mashed potatoes and a yam.
This year I'm going to help out, 'cause that's the kind of guy I am.
Deciding that I should make it as my Thanksgiving goal,
I'll cook up that tasty side dish, the green bean casserole.

I go to the supermart for greens beans and mushroom soup,
I don't want people to think that I am not in the loop.
I mix all the ingredients and then I add some cheese,
finish it off with the onion rings easy as you please.

I've seen this casserole before, this isn't how it looked,
maybe it will look a lot better after it is cooked.
I go ahead and cover it with that silvery foil,
I wrap it very tightly, I don't want it to spoil.

Yelling "I brought the green bean casserole" I walk in the door,
I topped it with French's cheese onion rings, who could ask for more.
The hostess sets it in the oven, so it can start to cook.
I tell her what kind of dish it is, she doesn't even look.

Taking it to the table she removes the foil top,
both my kids keep staring at it like they're some kind of cop.
Looking at their Gramma, in unison they cry, "What's this?"
By the way they're saying it, I feel something is amiss.

There's only one green bean in there, sitting on the side,
everybody turns toward me and I just want to hide.
The way they all are snickering hurts me deep in my soul,
if there should be more than one, call it GREEN BEANS
CASSEROLE!

MY LITTLE VAMPIRE

You sexy vampire, your tooth is so long,
and you're tempting me with your siren song.
As I look at you and your beautiful fang,
you are probably thinking I don't give a dang.

With sexy long legs and haunting blue eyes,
you think I'm falling for all of your lies.
People warned me about you, but I guess what the heck,
you can come here right now and chomp upon my neck.

Suck out a pint or two, I'll let you make the call,
all that I ask of you is do not take it all.
I would appreciate it if you'd let me know when you are done.
Then maybe we can get together and have a little fun.

You say you are feeling woozy and throwing up a lot?
You should see yourself in the mirror, oops, sorry, I forgot.
You think you might be dying, because you drank so much of my blood.
Well, I do eat lots of steaks and garlic, and lots of other crud

VALENTINE'S DAY PAST

I remember Valentines Day for what happened years ago,
it wasn't very pleasant, it was really quite a blow.
I fell in love with a pretty nurse whose hair was long and black.
She was the nicest girl I knew and was terrific in the sack.

I knew her for a few months when an idea filled my head.
I told my friends and family it was her I need to wed.
Everyone was happy for me, I finally found a mate.
She said yes when I asked her, so we went out and set a date.

Then fate played a trick on me, and I had a nasty heart attack.
The doctor said it was so bad, I was lucky to make it back.
They gave me a MIR and an electrocardiogram.
They said that in the pictures, my heart looks just like a honey ham.

I went on a transplant list so I could get on with my life,
and start up a new family with my soon to be new wife.
Then one day the doctor called to say that they have found a heart.
I should rush right to the hospital, they have it on a cart.

When I arrive and see the Doc, there was sadness on his face.
The nurse I loved, took the heart, and put a sucker in its' place.
I'm okay, I found out my tests were switched by that little tart.
I have to end this poem now, to look for the girl who stole my heart.

HIS REVENGE

Sitting at Christmas dinner with my green beans casserole,
I can't help from thinking if Santa's going to take control.
I must admit this happened in my younger days,
when I was going through the funny prankster stage.

I put pot into his cookies and EX-LAX in his milk.
The cookies were so tasty, they went down as smooth as silk.
After all the cookies, I knew he'd pour the milk down his throat.
I just sat back laughing so hard, I could not help but gloat.

I get this brand new tan coat, the tag says from Santa Claus.
But before I put it on, something makes me stop to pause.
I decide to try the damn thing on and it feels alright.
But, now I come to think of it, the arms are kind of tight.

The arms keep getting tighter and they wrap around the back
Suddenly I begin to feel I've come under attack.
Finally I'm wrapped up so tight I have to sit up straight,
tears are forming in my eyes, knowing I fell for the bait.

You know jolly Old St. Nick, the one that kids adore,
let me tell you something, he's not jolly anymore.
You have to remember that I did this when I was still a kid
I didn't think he'd ever figure out exactly what I did.

I did not think he realized just how low I had stooped,
and that I was the little imp who made him feel pooped.
Yes, for that one night of hell, he had me to thank.
I've been waiting 40 years for him to play a prank.

An ambulance pulls up in front, men in white coats jump out.
"We've come to take Bob Ford away" is what I hear them shout.
By now the arms on the jacket are so tight I cannot budge.
I guess that jolly Old St. Nick, can really hold a grudge.

Sitting in this padded cell, again tears form in my eyes.
I hear this loud laughing voice, it's one that I recognize.
The voice seems to be coming from a flying Christmas sleigh,
"It's because you gave me the runs, that they put you away."

A LITTLE IRISHMAN

I'm a little fellow, who stands about one foot three.
I am such a rascal, there's no one bad as me.
There is a group of us guys on the Emerald Isle.
We love to play tricks on folks, it always makes us smile.

I wear a dark green suit and a silly little hat,
I have a little beard and I guess I'm a little fat.
When my friends and I get together we get kind of bold.
We tell a bunch of people that we have a pot of gold.

I tell them that it's hidden at the end of a rainbow,
if they're fast enough to catch me, I'll show them where to go.
For a small fee I'll lead them to an even bigger pot.
The dummies all believe me, you should see how much I got.

Much to my surprise, fate took a funny little turn,
and I hate to admit it but I have some concern.
Because one of my fingers I now have tripped upon,
I guess I'll be forever known as a leper con.

SO CLOSE

I went on a vacation to the Emerald Isle,
the home of my ancestors always makes me smile.
While running through the many fields of Kelly green.
I spot the weirdest female I have ever seen.

She looks like a leprechaun, I thought they were only male.
I'll bet she has a pot of gold, I must catch her without fail.
I start chasing her through the fields and over walls,
her foot catches on a stone and the lady falls.

I jump on her, tie up her hands, but I don't want to be mean.
She is far and away, the ugliest elf I've ever seen.
She said her name is Angela and she has a lot of gold.
She wants to give it all to me because she is getting old.

I don't know if she is heaven's child or the devil's own,
is she just a sweet old lady or bad right to the bone.
She says all I have to do is to escort her to County Cork.
I smile and gladly agree to this, because I'm such a dork.

As we go walking down the road she starts the crying game,
sobbing how she will soon be poor and I'm the one to blame.
She thumbs her nose, sticks out her tongue, and runs the other way.
As I looked up to the sky it has turned to a dark gray.

We're suddenly surrounded by hundreds of lightning flashes,
I turn around and all I see is a pile of Angela's ashes.
All my dreams of sudden wealth have just gone up in smoke.
I start to laugh at what I think is a pretty punny joke.

I'm now leaving the Emerald Isle as broke as when I came.
No, I don't have the riches or any of the fame.
My dad said things could always be worse, I feel with that I must concur.
even though I'm burned up at Angela, I'm not as burned up as her.

So if you catch a leprechaun, make sure you keep it very close,
unless you want yours to end up like mine, a crunchy piece of toast.
Now my story's over and the only thing that I can say,
"Is to go and have yourself a Happy St. Patrick's Day."

HAPPY HALLOWEEN

Let me start this poem by saying, "Happy Halloween"
I'm going to tell you of the strange things that I've seen.
They came from this big haunted house we had down the street.
I noticed all this stuff when I went out for trick or treat.

Of course there was a Full Moon, which made it extra scary.
It didn't help that the house was next to a cemetery.
I see ghosts and hear some eerie noise coming from the graveyard.
To think it could scare some people, would not be all that hard.

The house is decorated with the colors orange and black,
and I had a weird feeling as I walked up with my sack.
Peeking into the front window, I see a big black cat,
the old woman who is holding it has a pointed hat.

Is she really ugly or is it just a scary mask,
trying to figure this all out is really quite a task.
Her long flowing black gown has me thinking that she's a witch,
but I'm not telling anyone because I'm not a snitch.

There is a very big cauldron in the living room,
that this woman's stirring with the end of her witch broom.
It has to be some magic potion or a Witch's Brew.
I want to run away but I'm fascinated by the view.

Standing tall on the table is a huge vampire bat.
The room fills with ghosts and goblins, what do you think of that?
Since there is a full moon a werewolf has to be in there.
As I start to run, I trip over the pumpkin on the stair.

I ignore the pain in my body and start to run like hell,
I do not what to be put under some weird witch's spell.
So if you hear of a haunted house, best that you stay clear,
'cause Lord knows what will happen to you, if you get too near.

HOLIDAY GREETINGS

A Merry Christmas and Happy New Year,
to all of my friends that I hold so dear.
May these holidays bring you nothing but glee.
Even though you'll be getting those bad jokes from me.

I found you can't have enough family or friends by your side.
For all the love and support they can often provide.
Thanks for the jokes and notes that you send,
to let me know that I am your friend.

I know you don't see or hear from me very much,
an e-mail is mostly the way I keep in touch.
I want you to know just how much that I care,
and how good it feels knowing you are all there.

I heard some bad news, that might make some of you tingle.
Santa fell in the fire, he's now known as Krisp Kringle.
He could not see right, the air was not real clear.
It was not heavy snow, but a lot of reindeer.

Personal

MY MIRROR IMAGE

As I looked into the mirror,
in my eye I could feel a tear.
My view of life is slightly jaded,
hard to admit my youth has faded.

I had a muscular chest when I was young,
but a terrible transformation has now begun.
I look at the mirror and say, "Whoa, Nellie!"
My chest has been slipping into my belly.

My hair has gone from charcoal black to gray,
while watching my youth slowly drift away.
This has really put me in some kind of terrible funk,
So I get out a bottle of booze and get stinking drunk.

Going back to the mirror, looking for a small ray of hope,
by drowning myself with liquor, I should be able to cope.
So I take a good look and what is it I see,
just that same old fat guy looking back at me.

Age can take an enormous toll,
if you don't stop and take control.
The only way you can improve your own beauty,
is to make it your obligation and duty.

So making up my mind to start to exercise and diet,
I don't know if it will work, but I am going to try it.
Because if I succeed and become a whole lot thinner,
I'll have accomplished something and feel like a winner.

TRY LAMAZE

This message that I am writing
to all you future ma's and pa's.
If you want your birth exciting,
try the method of La Maze.

For 6 weeks you go to your instructor's house
with a pillow in each of your hands.
Neighbors may look strangely at you and your spouse,
But together you both feel grand.

You learn how to breathe and exercise
and all that birth involves.
Well, pretty soon you will realize
the problems that it solves.

When early labor finally makes the scene
and you start that happy ride.
You will find both of you are quite serene
with your sweetheart by your side.

Going in the labor room, you'll understand
exactly what I have stated above.
Because when you take hold of your spouse's hand,
it's not a labor of pain, but of love.

The delivery room is your next stop,
pretty soon you'll be giving birth.
When you leave you will feel you're on top.
It's the greatest feeling on Earth.

Please tell me, is La Maze any good?
The question is asked of me and my wife.
When you get pregnant we think you should,
to feel part of the miracle of life.

A DEAD PARTY

I'm walking though the graveyard in the middle of the night,
some might say that I'm nervous, I would say I'm full of fright.
Looking farther up the lane, I see something that I dread,
it looks like two older folks, I believe that they are dead.

I ask in a quaking voice, "Are you two out here pruning?"
"What are you crazy sonny boy, we're just out here spooning.
We make our one comeback every year on our wedding date,
since we can only come out at night we're gonna stay up late.

The people in the graveyard have become our closest friends,
we exhume all the bodies and the harvest never ends.
There is a legend in this extremely quiet neighborhood,
about a guy named Bobbo, they say his parties are quite good.

It's our hundredth anniversary and we want to do it right."
"Wait, my nickname is Bobbo and I have finally seen the light.
You guys go, dig up your friends, make sure they wear party shoes,
tonight we are going to party and chase away their blues.

I go and buy two kegs of beer, some hot dogs and such.
I do not know what they can eat, probably not to much.
Mille is the hostess, Harry and I are called the hosts.
I'm getting quite excited as the graveyard fills with ghosts.

Harry's in a nice suit, Mille in a party colored dress,
there were never more good-looking ghosts, I really must confess.
Everyone is dancing hardy, having themselves quite a ball,
as the echoes of the laughter bounce off the graveyard wall.

As the night grew older and we approached sunrise,
the laughter now dies down and tears fill up their eyes.
As they hug and kiss and say good night, all that I can hear,
is people saying, "What a night, I'm coming back next year!"

The next night I probe the gravesites and sit down upon the banks.
You're not going to believe this, I heard a response of "Thanks"
Harry and Millie if your listening, thanks for next year's invite.
I'll make sure the party is ready but for now I'll say good night.

MY CAR TRIP

I don't know if you believe in God but let me give you a tip,
if you don't believe in him, get into your car and take a trip.
Head out west to Arizona or New Mexico.
Those are two of the states where surely you must go.

Driving back home from Phoenix I was feeling a little bad,
after looking at those mountains I no longer feel sad.
The symmetry of the mountains looks like they were carved by hand
some of them. are so darn similar they look like they were planned.

Coming out of Phoenix the mountains didn't have a lot of trees,
but the beauty of the formations almost brought me to my knees.
Sometimes when the sun was shining down on them just right,
the colors that came out of them were both bold and bright.

People who know me well, will tell you I am not a camera buff,
but if I had a camera that day, I couldn't have shot enough.
To see a group of Mesas with their flat tops all in a row,
the sunlight shining on them, gave off a lovely kind of glow.

As I headed farther east, the mountains filled with trees,
it was like a painted picure, pretty as you please.
Exiting the town of Globe, the roadsides were covered in pine.
when you were driving your car through it, the smell was mighty fine.

It wasn't some meteor that created these works of art,
and how it really came to pass I do not know where to start.
I have to think God used the wind and water as his magic brush,
it may have taken thousands of years but he wasn't in a rush.

I cannot begin to describe the majesty I saw,
and how all this beauty filled my heart with awe.
I have to admit that I had fallen from the Lord,
after what I saw today my faith has been restored.

MY CHIROPRACTOR

Dr. Nancy Cannon is the name of my chiropractor,
she can make my back sound just like a nuclear reactor.
Nancy, the receptionist, seems to be just like a kin.
no matter how busy Doc is, she always fits me in.

Nancy and Nancy seem like a daughter and her mother.
That is of course, unless they're picking on each other.
I go into a room to use the electric pulse machine,
it really doesn't hurt at all but the name sounds kinda mean

It helps relax the muscles from the bottom to the top.
So when she presses on my spine, the vertebrae all pop.
Then she has me turn over so I'm lying on my back,
at the vertebrae in my neck, she wants to take a crack.

In order to be sure no vertebrae are missed,
she firmly takes my head and gives a little twist.
When we hear the popping sound, we know the neck is finished.
When I move it side to side, the pain is now diminished.

The only thing left to do is work upon my shoulder,
because there's some numbness in it, that is what I told her.
I hold on to her elbow and look into her face,
She says, "Ready," pushes down and pops it back in place.

I came into the office bent, now I'm walking straight,
she askes me how I'm feeling, I say I'm feeling great.
If she ever needs a reference, I'll be there to back her.
She should be called "Smart Ritz" because she is a wise cracker.

HAPPY 12TH ANNIVERSARY

After 12 years of marriage I am writing this poem,
so I can tell you how much you make our house a home.
If I wrote down all the compliments that I overlook,
I wouldn't be writing a poem, I'd be writing a book.

You keep the house neat, though that may not sound very big,
but it's a difficult job when you're married to a pig.
You also do quite a few other chores,
like washing the windows and waxing the floors.

Of course as a cook you must be a winner,
'cause if you weren't, I'd be 15 pounds thinner.
We watched my waistline get four inches bigger,
but you still maintain a good looking figure.

You pay the bills and handle all of the money,
It's no easy task and you do it well honey.
Things haven't always been easy and I've caused you some pain,
but nevertheless, you seldom, if ever, complain.

The way that I'm feeling there can be no denyin',
our greatest accomplishments are Kelly and Brian.
There is no question, there are no maybes,
together we make beautiful babies.

You clean up the kids when they're covered with dirt,
and help ease the pain when they fall and get hurt.
When the kids need a driver you give them a lift,
when presents need buying you will find the right gift.

If you're dressed real sexy or dressed like Bugs Bunny,
I want you to know that I still love you, honey.
You're really the woman that I still adore,
although you don't laugh at my jokes anymore.

There have been lots of memories through the years,
some of them brought laughter, some of them brought tears.
We've had some problems, but we worked them all out,
now we know what true love is really about.

People asked me to name the best day of my life,
I simply answer, the day I made you my wife.
So to thank you for taking this low paying job,
I say Happy Anniversary from your husband, Bob

MY DAUGHTER KELLY

My daughter Kelly has just became a teen,
quite a young lady, if you know what I mean.
Her long brown hair and those flashing blue eyes,
are going to attract a lot of guys.

But do I look worried? No, I am doing just fine,
I plan to lock her in her room till she's 29.
Cause she might be a young lady with her hair in a curl,
but to her father, she will always be his little girl.

I think of a round little baby, chubby of cheek,
of course, she lost most of that when she learned how to speak.
Or of the little girl dressed as a princess or bride,
that made both of her parents' hearts swell with pride.

The only time she rushes is when she's going to the mall,
then Kelly gets her rear in gear and she really gives her all.
She would gladly check out a store from the bottom to the top,
besides all her other qualities the girl was born to shop.

She likes to write poems and stories, on a little note pad,
their almost as good as the ones written by her Dad.
I'm sure as far as she's concerned, there is no one like her brother,
except when she needs someone to fight with, then she has her mother

The times we spent in Palatine, as she jumped from place to place,
or other spots we sat and watched as she twirled with style and grace.
Sometimes the things we do for our children sets up a hectic pace,
but it really doesn't matter, when you see the pride that's in their face.

Kelly likes to style hair and use different kinds of make-up,
her Mom would let her do things, if Kelly she could wake up.
but getting Kelly out of her bed,
is more like raising up the dead.

One of Kelly's other great loves,
extends from cats all the way to doves.
You know the girl's heart just sings,
if it has a tail, some fins or wings

If thru Kelly's teen age years, we are able to survive,
we might let her out of her bedroom when she's 25.
Well this poem is over, I'm not lyin',
Happy 13th from Mom, Dad and Brian.

BRIAN AND MELISSA'S WEDDING

When Brian and Melissa decided to wed,
this great idea came up inside of their head.
Let's see if we can marry somewhere on a beach.
Hopefully it's a goal they'll be able to reach.

So they went onto the Internet to search high and low,
deciding Captiva Island was the place they should go.
They did all they had to, to book rooms for their guests.
Got them airline tickets, then at last they could rest.

January the 1st was to be this couple's big day.
They wanted to start the new year in their own special way.
Kelly came over to fix Melissa's hair,
She made the curls extra tight so they would stay there.

She made them so darn tight, it is no baloney,
Melissa's head was sore for the ceremony.
Having close friends near was all part of their plan,
so there was Becca, Cassie, Matt, Mark and Dan.

Melissa's whole family was there, Gina, Mike, Jake and Kimmy.
Jim and Paula her parents, and let us not forget Jimmy.
Brian's family was there too, Kelly and Robb,
as were both his parents Kathy and Bob.

The bride was dressed in a gown of pure white,
and in it she was a beautiful sight.
Melissa and Brian exchanged vows of love,
asking for a blessing by God up above.

Then they took pictures of the bride and groom on the beach,
when Melissa sat on the sand you could hear women screech.
Why did he sit her on the sand with her white dress?
When she gets up it's going to be just a mess.

There was a nice dinner with the new bride and groom,
inside a cute little restaurant's small dining room.
I am ending this poem and the only thing I can say,
everyone wants to thank you for the beautiful day.

KELLY'S WEDDING

Friday, September 19th, in the year 2003
will be an important day for my family and me.
What's happening on that day, at 3:30 on the dot,
Kelly and her fiancé Rob are going to tie the knot.

All their friends and relatives came together at the site,
to watch a ceremony that was truly a delight.
Lindsey as the Maid of Honor and Jamie the Bridesmaid,
the image of their beauty from my mind will never fade.

Looking up the aisle at Rob standing in his tux,
I'm thinking that he's looking like a million bucks.
Jim, the Best Man, is Rob's brother, Groomsman Jason, his good
friend.
How they could look any better I cannot comprehend.

Brian, Kelly's brother, and Joey, Jamie's beau, ushered people in,
How good looking they both were, I don't know where to begin.
so everyone in the party had an elegance and charm,
either walking up by themselves or with someone on their arm.

Barbara and Jim, his parents, Vicky and Mike both their spouses,
along with Kathy and Bob was the meeting of three houses.
The McGinley's, Ford's, Bilek's and Wallace's were family of the bride.
While the Paul's, Mirsch's and Mueller's were the names filling up his
side.

As our turn comes to walk down the aisle my heart fills with pride.
I'll be next to Kelly, who makes a most beautiful bride.
I didn't realize to the father it's a mixed emotions day,
because your heart is filled with pride and joy, then you "give" your girl
away.

Everything at the reception turned out as it should,
the food and the services both were very good.
The room with its chandeliers and mirrored wall,
made it just an outstanding reception hall.

As for the DJ and his music who could ask for more,
'cause his selection of music had people on the floor.
However my praise of him can only go so far,
because you must remember we had an open bar.

I think I speak for everyone when I say,
thank you for sharing this very special day.
So as you start your journey of new husband and new wife,
know that all your friends and families wish you both the best is life.

Gross

I'M POOPED

I had some constipation, I couldn't take a shit.
I went and bought some Ex-Lax to help get rid of it.
I took a healthy dose of it then waited over night,
when I got up the next morning there were no turds in sight.

So I took another dose of it, now I am passing gas,
due to the size of the explosions I think I cracked my ass.
I've been named by my kids as the "Father of the Fart"
I pass gas so often, it's called a form of art.

I feel no movement in my stool, again, a large dose I take.
As I take a look back on it now, that was a big mistake.
Now my bowel movements have a look of brownish pee.
I'm telling you right now, it's something you don't want to see.

Sitting here on the toilet, I am really getting mad.
It has to be the worst case of "runs" I have ever had.
Then into my life, I receive yet another blow,
an invite to a party, to which I have to go.

What I think I should do is stick a cork into my butt.
I know what you must be thinking, "Is he some kind of nut?"
So I got myself all dressed up and went to the party,
got me some food and drink and I'm feeling kind of farty.

Now I'm as sorry as sorry can be.
The blast killed two and injured more than three.
They said what really killed them, wasn't just the peat.
But the blast that was behind it blew them 40 feet.

So I sit in this lonely cell, waiting for my trial.
I know this sounds crazy, but I crack a little smile.
I put some Ex-Lax in my shorts, I want to make it very clear.
I may need it later, so I can blast my way out of here.

So, if you're taking Ex-Lax, be careful if you can,
I just told you what happens when shits hits the man.
The thing is you don't know who it hits, family or friend,
But just like this poem right now, it surely means "The End"

A LITTLE SNOT

I'm a little boogie inside my owner's nose,
I have to hold on tightly, when his nose he blows.
I am staying in here whether he likes it or not,
I'm not going anywhere 'cause I'm a little snot.

Sometimes he does his best to try to pick me out,
by placing his finger deep up inside his snout.
If he gets lucky, he might get a piece of me.
But there is so much of me that he does not see.

If I feel runny, I try not to let him know,
'cause if he blows at that point, I usually have to go.
But even if he does that, I'm pretty safe you see,
most of me is hiding in his sinus cavity.

When I finally dry out, again a booger I become,
I call up a few more booger friends, then we have some fun.
We all get together and clog up his nose like we should,
When we go and do that our owner doesn't breathe so good.

What is going on, is he using some nasal spray?
Is he trying to break us up so we cannot play?
Actually this angers me, I am getting very hot.
I'll find a way to get him back, 'cause I'm a little snot

SNEEZES

I don't know what was in the air on that hot summer day,
whether it was all the pollen or just a lot of hay.
It got me to thinking how people sneeze in different ways.
Is it a real habit or maybe it's just a phase.

There are the people who before the sneeze attacks,
tightly hold their nose and it blows out their ear wax.
Is it done for a reason or is it just in fear?
Why anyone would do this, really is not that clear.

Apparently they're embarrassed 'cause they have to sneeze,
they go through such contortions they buckle at the knees.
Don't they realize what they're doing is committing suicide,
'cause when they plug up their nose like that all the germs blow back
inside.

It makes me think of another special kind of sneeze.
I call it the "Wet One" 'cause it hangs like melting cheese.
You know the one I'm talking about, when your nose is runny.
You let it go, the booger hangs, it's really kind of funny.

Then there are those people who sneezes sound just like a toot.
They try to hold it back at the end, they really are a hoot.
People who can hold back like that, have it down to such an art.
You want to ask, "Was that a sneeze or did you just pop a fart?"

Now we'll talk about the sneeze you'd call normal I suppose.
When you hear a little noise, then the person wipes his nose.
About this kind of sneeze, there's not much you can say.
The people feel better than just go on their way.

If you know of a sneezer who has what I call "The Blast,"
when you see him start to sneeze better grab hold of something fast.
The force of air behind these can knock books right off of the shelves.
These make a mess of other people and the sneezers themselves.

ODE TO DE FART

My mind has gone from snot to diarrhea, that is how it starts.
Now I can't stop myself from thinking of the different kinds of farts.
I don't know if anybody out there really cares,
about the horrid smells around people's derrieres.

There's the silent but deadly type that we all know has no sound,
unless they admit to it, there's no way the owner can be found.
It takes over a room like an oncoming fog,
these are the kind of farts you blame upon the dog.

Then there is the fart that I like to call "The Oops"
when you go to pass it, out comes some of the poops.
These are the kind if your sitting down in a chair,
leaves a little brown spot on your underwear.

Now I want to talk about the one I called "The Doosey"
smelling this is so bad it makes people feel woosey.
That's the one when nature finally calls,
it peels the paper right off the bathroom walls.

We all know the kind of fart that I like to call "The Squeaker"
makes the same sound when you walk on wet tile with a sneaker.
I think I know the reason why you hear the squeaks,
it's because the gas comes out through moving butt cheeks.

No one can forget the one I like to call "The Blast,"
it's the kind of fart that leaves people all aghast.
If you pass one like that while sitting in a chair,
you're going to go flying two feet in the air.

The last time I heard a woman fart? I don't know how long it's been.
I don't know how they do it, but they somehow manage to keep it in.
If I don't pass when I have to, my body starts to swell,
then when I finally let it go, it really stinks like hell.

I do not talk a lot about the last one, I call it "The Mush."
It's when you go to fart and diarrhea blows out your tush.
I'm going to finish this poem now and as I depart,
I've decide to name this nonsense an "Ode to de Fart."

Punny Stories

A TRIP TO THE ZOO

I love animals. I have two dogs of my own. I used to have a cat but I lost her. I only pay so much for a cat. Yes, I have a fee line.

Today I'm going to the zoo to see the animals there. The first one I come to is a big hairy thing. I can see why he's called Grizzly but why is he called bear?

There's two large deer in a huge pen. One's standing by himself he must be a stag. The other stag must be rich, looks like he has a lot of doe around him. The baby goat running around is looking for his nanny, I guess. A little boy comes up to me and asks me if I've seen his uncle, "No, but I've seen a lot of ants."

I go by the big cats. There's the one who never tells the truth, that's a lion. The other one roaming the area doesn't play fair, he's a cheetah. The striped animal with something around his neck that's always growing, has to be a tiger.

It's getting hot so I've got to move faster, it's so hot I can see a camel smoking, Someone said giraffes are great lovers because they like a good long neck. The ducks at this zoo are so smart they tell jokes, they're a bunch of wise quackers.

I need to take a break, so I see this nice building. I go there and it's a place where you can watch serious plays and have milk and cheese. They call it a drama dairy. As I come out there are two insects flying around a hive. Is it 2 bees or not 2 bees, that is the question? I need to know I'm allergic to bees.

A commotion was starting a little bit a way. I found out it was a Friar who was locked out of his monastery. He was looking for a Monk key.

Then I see people trying to keep this bird from getting a drink. He must be a Myna. I see a dog chasing other dogs, knocking them down and kissing them. That's no dog, it's a wolf. The animal over there is smiling and slowly shaking his head from side to side. this has to be a Rhino.

My last stop is the sea aquarium. I pick up a crab from the beach they had there. It pooped in my hands, I didn't care, it was a gift from sandy claws. There were some big fish in the water that weren't moving. They didn't have shiny scales like most fish. That means they were either sick or dull fins.

As I left, I found out which animal has the largest breast—the Zebra

A PLAY ON WORDS

I was standing by my picture window, when I realized I was in a lot of pane. I saw my two neighbors standing across the street, they were mad. I knew they were going to cross because they couldn't curb their anger.

I didn't know who they were at first, but the man's head kept going up and down, so I figured it must be Bob. The pregnant woman on crutches would be his wife Mame. I didn't know she was an actress, but I could see she was in a cast.

She got down on her hands and knees and pounded on the door. She's always knocked up. They say they're going to sue me because her leg is broken. "Why blame me?" I asked. She said "Your dog was barking and I fell from the woof." My dog was laying down. I looked at her, she got up, and I can see her paws." You have no proof, and stay away from my house because you've become an eavesdopper.

I told them to go back home and Bob walked right into some trees. I yelled, "Their bark is worse then their bite," so he gets up and leaves. That was a while ago, they're divorced now. She won the lawsuit because she's still on crutches. I guess she can support herself. You may think this story was staged because it's a play on words.

A PLAY ON WORDS PART TWO

It's summertime and I need to get a few things done. I knew I was going to need some money. So I went boating by myself. I turned off the motor and drifted to the Seashore Banks, I needed to float alone. I tried to spot someone like myself. I was trying to find a peer.

I needed to relax, so I went fishing for salmon with my two dogs. I was pulling them in left and right. They were falling on the dogs. It made me hungry looking at the lox and beagles.
I was scaling one of the fishes when he got away, it cost me a fin. I heard of a woman who lost her scale, now she can't find her weigh. I guess she'll just have to wait.

I decided to finish my shopping while I was out. I went to the Home Depot store to pick up some wood, I was bored. Some of the wood had holes, I guess they were bored too. I was so confused about putting something next to my windows. Every time I visualized it, I shuttered.

After that, I went to the store to get 4 new radials for my truck. The man at the store said I could only afford the front ones. I didn't argue, I was just to tired.

I told you about Bob and Mame last time. My new neighbor is always lugging things around, his name is Cary. His wife is a whiner and staggers when she walks, her name is Sherry.

Cary built beautiful large homes, trouble is, they all fell down after 2 months, he was arrested for bad Manors. He put gold in all the exit portals and called them the great out doors. The telephone company had him put in jail, now he can only use a cell phone.

His brother was always digging holes, his name is either Barry or Doug. He was a dirty old man, till he fell into some soap and water, now he's just washed up. I heard he kissed a male deer, he'll do anything for a buck.

His wife is very outgoing and happy, she's named Mary or Joy. She was an actress in a road play. Whenever she was working on the play, she became a cast away.

This story stinks like a football lineman's armpit, maybe I should call it Right Guard.

I LOVE SPORTS

Don't ever move in with a woman unless you know her well. I made that mistake, after I moved in, she told me she hated sports. Didn't like to watch them, didn't even like to talk about them. I reluctantly agreed. She asked me what I had in the bank. I said, "Nothing but net." She said, "Are you taking a shot at me?" I said, "That's not my goal." "That's all you ever think or talk about." "Not true, sex is what I always think about."

I promised I wouldn't use any more sports terms. I asked her if she'd like to see 'Mac Beth' and 'Chicago.' She said, "That's a double play!" I told her she was driving me batty. I said, "How could I ever feel safe with you?" "Aren't you happy with the sacrifice I made?" "More baseball talk!" she said. I could tell she was teed off. I calmed her down and we headed for the bedroom. I needed to go to the bathroom real fast, I told her it would be a short stop. When we got in bed I grabbed the pillow, I love the feel of feathers. Yes, I love to touch down.

When we got undressed she put her clothes on a hanger, all I got was a left and right hook. As she was taking off her nylons, her finger poked through. I shouted, "You made a hole in one!" I guess she wasn't feeling up to par. She starts to cry and keeps hitting me. She hit me so hard the one time I stared seeing birdies. I yell out, "No more bawls and strikes! I'm trying to steal your heart, but you won't let me get to first base.

The next night I told her she was making me nervous. I was getting the 'runs' because of her and her hatred of sports. She said, "Give me your best pitch." That threw me a curve, so I stuck out at her verbally. She said, "Don't use foul language on me!" I didn't think the language was bad but she told me I crossed the foul line.

We decided to eat dinner and calm down. I wanted someone to taste the hot drink she gave me, I thought she might have poisoned it. I wanted a safe tea. Since there was no one there I took a punch from the refrigerator. I brought some dessert home, as I look back on it now, not a good idea. Why? It was a Bundt cake with icing. I thought she'd have a stroke. She told me to leave, so I went back to live with my parents. She thought she threw me out but I knew I was safe a home.

You know, I never realized how much I use sports terms when I talked, until I read this.